RADICAL LINES

from a

LIT CITY

by Bob-Davis

Jim,
Best of luck in your new
adventures !!! I hope you
like the book !
Bob-Davis

For Paul Swart
who never lost faith in me

and

Bill and Jayne Davis
for their love and support

Acknowledgements

I am very grateful to the following family and friends for their support as funders and contributors. Without their help, this book may not have become a reality.

Funders

Karen and Jay Argus, Robert Betis and Aaron True, Joseph Cofrancesco, Alexis D'Angelo, Alfred and Denise D'Angelo, Andrew D'Angelo, Stephanie D'Angelo, William and Jayne Davis, Joanne Delahanty, Linda Delahanty and Paul Gorski, Jamie and Philip Desjardins, Anne El Shazli, Paul Endry, Matthew Fraiden, Adrienne Haspel, Nicolas Hell, Andre Henderson, Helen Higginbotham, Jailan Ismail, George Lombardo, Bilal Mazhar, Blair and Erin Miles, Lee Polansky, Mario Rey, Paul Swart, Roza Vasileva, Elnur and Heather Veliev, Peter Vickers

Story Contributors

Boomie Aglietti
David Jaggard
James H. Jewell III
Antonia Alexandra Klimenko
Moe Seager
David Leo Sirois

4

Contents

Preface   9

Gertrude's Stepson   11

Chapter 1 – Paris   13

Chapter 2 – Je suis un appareil-photo 1   31

Culture Rapide   33
Looking-Glass Bottles   34
Fontaine de la place Gambetta   35
Renewal   36
Revolutionarias   37
Carousel - Marais   38
Adults of Anarchy   39
Mannequins of Color   40
The Scourge of Paris   41
She Is   42

Chapter 3 – Satire in Prose   43

Mixed Metaphors, or Optimism   45
Nightmare on Facebook   48
Bastille Day: A Half-Baked History   52
Clean Conceptions   55
The Case of the Perrimasons   57
B-Boy   60
The Church of J. Christ, Banker   64
A Movie Made in Heaven   67
An All Hallowed Eve's Carol   71
Saints and Snakes of the Emerald Isle   73
Boatloads   76
Vat's in a Name?   78
Forever Noir   80
For the Love of God   83
And Then There Were Nine   86

Chapter 4 – Americans in Paris   89

A Sweeping Entrance
       by Antonia Alexandra Klimenko   92
The Accidental Gendarme
       by Boomie Aglietti   95
Ode to Jouissance
       by David Jaggard   96
Queen of Beggars
       by David Leo Sirois   98
Rain Near the Old Road
       by James H. Jewell III   100
Dinner with the In-laws
       by Moe Seager   102

Chapter 5 – Je suis un appareil-photo 2   107

Joie de Nutella   109
Closed Door   110
Rue Dénoyez   111
Princes of Paris   112
Obsessive Compulsive   113
Time-Framed   114
Ice Facades   115
In Memoriam   116
Regurgitation   117
Art Nouveau/Vieux   118
Sun, Sand, Seine   119

Chapter 6 – Satire in Verse   121

Psalm DCLXVI   123
Poetic Complacency   125
Fleeting Essentials   127
Nothing to Do   128
The American Plan   130
Pride for Prejudice   132
La Rime   133
The Blues in Rhyme   134

by DesigN   136
Ergo Sum, Ergo Sum Non   138
Avant-garde   140
Fundamental Wails   142
Cut and Paste   144

Chapter 7 – Satire in Life   147

Behind in Sight   149
The Thorazine Years, Part I   151
The Thorazine Years, Part II   153
Dramatis Personae   155

Endquotes   157

About the Author   158

Preface

Satire: the use of humor, irony, exaggeration, or ridicule to expose and criticize people's stupidity or vices, particularly in the context of contemporary politics and other topical issues.
The Apple Mac Dictionary

I have been writing and performing for many years but always as an avocation. After too many years of working in unfulfilling jobs, I thought it was about time to make a change and pursue a creative vocation. My favorite literary genre is satire. I have written satirical pieces, and the occasional poem, for many years but this is my first attempt at a book. I credit my inspiration to the imaginative atmosphere of Paris.

Living in Paris has re-awakened my desire to write. While many of these stories and poems are "American" in nature, more than 80% of the material was written, and the remainder significantly rewritten, in Paris. There are several stories about Paris and the Parisians and many of the pieces allude to French writers and French literature. The poetry selections were developed over a year in the company of many budding poets. One of the poems is in French. The twenty-one color photographs offer a unique view of the city. I have also included humorous anecdotes by six American writers who currently live in Paris. I think the spirit of Paris can be felt throughout the book. Additionally, I have included a few personal pieces from my unconventional life that I felt were germane to the parody of life in which I live.

Charlie Hebdo

On Wednesday, January 7, were the brutal attacks and murders of the staff at the satiric newspaper, Charlie Hebdo and also at a kosher Jewish supermarket. A few Muslim jihadists killed seventeen people. It was a horrific act that instilled fear in the citizens of Paris and anxiety about possible future attacks. Makeshift memorials popped up around the city and there were several vigils to commemorate the murder victims. On Sunday, January 11, there was a huge march from Place de la République to Place de la Nation. The crowd was guesstimated at over one million people.

Many have claimed that the attacks were not really about religion so much as the marginalization and powerlessness of the Arab minority in both Paris and all of France. I believe that religion was the primary factor in these senseless attacks. Shouts of "Allahu Akbar" are not actions of the irreligious. Many of these jihadists are young people who naively accept the tenets of radical Islam as truth and as a rationale for violence and "martyrdom." In reality, they are merely examples of unnecessarily wasted lives.

I believe that religious organizations and religious beliefs are detrimental aspects of society. Growing up as a gay man in the Catholic Church, I was taught to think of myself as a sinner who defies the word of God and who would eventually end up in hell. Even in 2015, they continue to malign LGBT people. This malicious behavior of the church was evident during the initial AIDS crisis in the 1980s and 90s as religious leaders joined the chorus of nasty comments such as, "This is God's punishment for gays," and "They deserve what they get." Religious organizations were also slow in providing any care to the gay men who were dying horrific deaths.

Religion and politics have long been my favorite satirical targets. Both areas of society are all about money, power, deception, and corruption. The folly of "spiritual" beliefs and the unscrupulous behavior of politicians provide endless material for the satirist. Mark Twain succinctly summed up the chicanery of the powers that be:

"I am quite sure now that often, very often, in matters concerning religion and politics a man's reasoning powers are not above the monkey's."

I hope this collection gives you a few laughs and/or a few tears. Throw away the daily meditations, dispense with the daily newspaper and ditch the erotica. Start your day off with a smirk and a sneer – straight from Paris to you.

Bonne lecture!

Gertrude's Stepson

At last I see Paris

Not the one of Stein and Hemingway

Or Beckett and Baldwin

The Paris I see is all mine

Harking to me like nimble sirens of old

Eerily seducing me with that transcendent charm

Rendering me helpless in her presence

And yet, I grow stronger

Mesmerized by beauty, elegance, joie de vivre

Enmeshed in an unabashed world of aesthetic eruptions

Reinvented and reformulated with each passing decade

Into that juxtaposition of antiquity and modernity

Creativity exudes from her pores like No. 5 on a little black dress

And so too must I ooze such fragrant originality

No more desperate paperwork in a cubicle of despair

I can't kill what tiny shards of soul I may have left

Nor forsake a latent career as I have yet to have one

And what better place than the heart of Europe

Rimbaud, Cocteau, Sartre, Saint-Exupéry

I descend into enchantment like a sprite

Savoring it like a robust cabernet.

"Being a Parisian is not about being born in Paris,
it is about being reborn there."
Sacha Guitry

PARIS

"To breathe Paris is to preserve one's soul."
Victor Hugo

American humorist David Sedaris made the following observation about Paris:

"In Paris the cashiers sit rather than stand. They run your goods over a scanner, tally up the price, and then ask you for exact change. The story they give is that there aren't enough euros to go around … I think the real problem lies with the Parisian cashiers, who are, in a word, lazy." (from *When You Are Engulfed in Flames*)

I have lived in Paris for a year now. I go to the supermarket regularly and in my experience, what Sedaris says about Parisian cashiers is true. It takes longer to get through the checkout line than to do the shopping. When I mentioned this to a Parisian friend, she just looked at me and said, "You're in Paris!" I find it difficult to see many flaws in the French capital. Mr. Sedaris has lived in Paris for many years and he is by no means a Francophobe as evidenced in this next comment:

"There's a section [in *Paris to the Moon*] where he's talking about crossing the Pont Neuf at sunset on a winter's evening. And he talks about how the beauty of it just absolutely stops him and stops his heart. I remember when I read that it made me cry. I copied it down in my diary because it was the perfect description of that feeling and of that time of day. And Paris is so beautiful that, even after 10 years, I stop sometimes and I am just overwhelmed." (from July 2008 interview in *The Globe and Mail*)

This is the Paris that seduced me many years ago when I first came here for a summer study program. I still see this magical city through those adolescent eyes. There's nothing like being able to drink wine and smoke cigarettes with abandon at sixteen. To this day I still consider it blasphemy to sit in a Parisian cafe without a glass of wine and a Gauloises.

I have always wanted to live in Paris but my returns were only for short visits. Back in 2000, I made an attempt to live in the city but due to a complete lack of any plan, my effort was in vain. Finally, after more years of tedious jobs, a law school degree, and living in the comparatively sterile environment of Washington, DC, I finally took the plunge in September 2013. It was the best move I have ever made. I grew up in Boston and I have lived in Washington, DC, San Francisco, and Los Angeles but Paris is the only city where I feel truly at home, like I finally belong somewhere.

During my year in Paris, I have stayed in two apartments that I found through one of the vacation rental sites. Both apartments are in the 20th arrondissement in the eastern end of Paris, not too far from the well-known Père Lachaise cemetery. The first apartment was tiny, about 180 sq. ft. Unfortunately the apartment had not been cleaned before I arrived so, much to my chagrin, I was forced to do some cleaning right off the bat. But even worse, someone with long, dark hair had been the previous occupant and there were strands of hair everywhere. Happily, I was only in that apartment for three weeks.

Shortly after my arrival, I began writing a blog called The Bob-World (www.the-bob-world.com). The blog includes my adventures in Paris, my writings, photographs from performances, amusing quotes, and a variety of special features. I have maintained the blog up to the present. I actually decided to write this book after receiving positive feedback about the blog from my small but devoted cadre of readers.

My second Paris apartment is larger (225 sq. ft.), very clean, and has a nice sized bathroom and kitchen, Wi-Fi (pronounced wee-fee in French), and, best of all, a washing machine. It is a very French neighborhood, few tourists, and convenient. Nearby, there are two metro stops, five supermarkets, three *boulangeries* (bread stores), three *tabacs*, cafes and restaurants — all within six blocks. Twice each week, there is a large open-air market near the metro that sells everything from fresh produce to nail clippers.

Paris has always been a city of small, specialized stores and open-air markets. While this is still the norm, the American Empire has saturated the city with fast-food restaurants and retail chain stores. I will note, however, that one good thing about McDonald's when traveling in a foreign country, is that it always has clean bathrooms, soda with ice, and relatively large coffees.

There truly is no joy like a freshly baked baguette from the *boulangerie* with a touch of butter and strawberry jam. It really is in one of those ecstatic realms. The accompanying coffee is also delicious – even the instant kind. The dark chocolate (three bars for less than two dollars) is excellent and good wine can be had for under ten dollars.

I find the Parisians to be quite friendly to those who make an effort to speak French. When a French person initially encounters me, English is immediately attempted on the assumption that I am English or American and unable to speak French. I must have an American flag tattooed to my forehead that only the French can see. Most Parisians speak some English. They all study it in school but many seem to feel that their English skills are poor and are hesitant to use them. There is also the myth that the French do not like Americans but, in my experience, they love both America and Americans. Our music, films, television, and fashions can be found everywhere.

It cannot be reiterated enough how beautiful the architecture is in this city. The French also have a knack for combining the old with the modern in such as way as to create a seamless connection between the two. A prime example is the glass pyramid designed by I. M. Pei as the entrance to the Louvre. The glass pyramid only enhances the centuries-old palace. There is also a good deal of construction going on throughout the city as Paris morphs into her next incarnation.

Le métro

I love the Paris subway or *le métro*. The trains arrive every four minutes (six on Sundays and holidays). There is a convenient and reasonably priced monthly pass called the *Passe Navigo*. In what I consider to be a strange twist, there are very few elevators in the subway system. It is not user-friendly for anyone who is physically challenged. I knew I was on my way to becoming a Parisian when a young guy asked me for metro directions. On another occasion, I heard the bell of an incoming train. I raced to catch it and took a head dive down the stairs to the amusement and/or concern of the subway riders. Having fallen many times over the years, or what I like to call "tumbling," I am very good at it. Generally, I jump right up in complete embarrassment and hope that not too many people have witnessed my acrobatics. So far, I have gotten away with only skinned knees but I can foresee the all-too-common broken hip or two in the not-too-distant future.

I have also been reminded that when asking directions, it is necessary to ask at least three people in order to get a simple majority with actual knowledge of the city. I also find this to be true wherever I go. For whatever reason, I am frequently asked for directions, even in Paris. If I don't know the directions for the requested destination, I am not ashamed to admit that unlike many others! I was a concierge in Los Angeles for several years and I must appear to have an aura of geography about me.

Excercise

I found what I think is the only reasonably priced gym in the city called Neoness. It's only two years old and costs twenty dollars per month with restricted but sufficient hours. Between the gym, a lot of walking and the healthier food in France, I have managed to lose some weight while still enjoying bread and butter, creamy sauces, and the most incredible chocolate, custard/crème anglaise, and cream-filled desserts.

I quickly realized that the two pairs of sneakers I brought with me were too old and worn to handle much walking and they were killing my feet. It was time to go shopping. I visited several shoe stores and tried on about a dozen pairs of sneakers. None of them fit. My feet have been the same large size since the sixth grade where all my classmates were in hysterics when I came in with new shoes. Here, in one of the shoe capitals of the world, the glass slipper just doesn't fit. As I headed toward the gay Marais, I found a Nike store. I went in and the friendly salesman was excited about this challenge. The next thing I knew I was walking out wearing a pair of Nike Kevin Durant "Meteorology" sneakers which had just arrived that morning. I had no idea who Kevin Durant is but the sneakers not only fit but they were also a bit stylish. As I walked through the Marais it seemed that everyone was staring at my pink, black and grey fashion statement.

Singularités

Every city has its quirks. There are many idiosyncrasies about Paris

18

that I have noticed over this longer span of time.

It rains constantly but umbrellas can be had a cheap price.

Pigeons dominate the city with the accompanying ramifications.

Carousels seem to be very popular here and the colorful amusement rides can be found throughout the city.

There are many holidays celebrated here, mostly religious ones. Despite a plethora of churches in the city, the Parisians are not necessarily devout but they do love their holidays, religious or otherwise.

Nutella is immensely popular here. There is competition from smaller companies and every supermarket carries their own version. I can testify that it tastes pretty darn good on a slice of baguette. I do have to limit my purchases of the tasty spread, as I tend to eat it straight from the jar with a spoon!

Scarves are extremely popular and sometimes they are the only colorful accessories to the *de rigeur* black outfits. Regardless of the weather, the donning of a scarf is never inappropriate.

I was unable to find Tums or any comparable antacids for a bout of indigestion. I only found something similar to Prevacid for about twenty dollars.

The cost of a hamburger at many restaurants also costs twenty dollars.

The sidewalks of Paris are narrow and the Parisians would just as soon run into you as let you by. I did learn that if you wait till the very last second, he or she will move. To be fair, I often see similar behavior on Connecticut Avenue in DC.

Paris continues to empty out during the month of August, save for the tourists, and many retail stores are closed for the entire month. My French open mic was suspended for the entire month and my gym was closed for two weeks.

I have been to Paris enough that I have seen most of the usual tourist sights include many of the museums. But over the last year I have revisited some of the more interesting venues. The famously dead Père Lachaise cemetery is within walking distance from my apartment. Among those resting there are Oscar Wilde, Gertrude Stein, Edith Piaf, Molière, Jim Morrison, Frédéric Chopin, Jacques-Louis David, and Marcel Proust. Whenever I go to the cemetery, there are never any maps available making it difficult to find the famous gravesites. I once asked the guard when they will have maps again and she replied, "When they are delivered." Gotta love that French irony.

I visited the Paris Museum of Modern Art on a couple occasions. Admittance is always free. It seemed strange to be looking at Picassos and Matisses but I guess that's because I rarely go to art museums at home. I have yet to acquire a taste for cubism. I already have sufficient surrealism in my life. Many of the newer avant-garde works could be called "bleeding edge," not unlike the pictures that Phoebe Buffay created with arms, legs, furniture or musical instruments protruding from the canvas. (Please note the bizarre parallels between fine art and sitcoms.)

There is a special two-for-one pass to see both the Musée d'Orsay and the Musée de l'Orangerie. At the Musée d'Orsay was an exhibit called Masculin/Masculin, a collection of male nudes painted or sculpted over the centuries. I can safely say that it was a pretty hot exhibit. The Musée de l'Orangerie has a lot of big names including Monet, Cezanne, Picasso, and Renoir. I don't get cubism at all! At that time they were showing an exhibit on the husband/wife team of Frida Kahlo and Diego Rivera. I do have to admit that my maximum tolerance at art museums is about two hours.

My final sightseeing venture was a return to the palace of Versailles. I think it had been over twenty years since my last visit. The opulence and enormity of the palace are in the sphere of hyperbole. I could easily have lived quite comfortably in either the Hall of Mirrors or the Queen's bedroom. I think the overriding theme was that the very wealthy have always raped their surroundings, kept people in servitude and did little to benefit anyone but themselves. The 1% in the seventeenth century was not much different from the 1% today.

On Bastille Day, I attended a picnic with a group of English-speaking writers at the Champ de Mars in front of the Eiffel Tower before the fireworks began. I don't think I have ever seen such a stunning display of pyrotechnics. Every summer there is a music festival, Fête de la Musique, throughout the city of Paris. There are musicians, singers and bands of every musical genre performing in large and small clubs and restaurants as well as the streets and parks. Two friends, Peter Deaves (aka Fun King Nero) and Petra Titawano performed in the festival at a brasserie in the Latin Quarter.

During October 2013, I did venture to the south of France, specifically, Nice and Montpellier. I had been to Nice years ago and it was pleasant to visit again. The views of the Mediterranean are still beautiful and the weather is great. I found a gay leather bar there that I thought might be interesting but, sadly, it was quite uneventful and scarcely populated. But, Nice is nice! (Sorry, I just had to!)

I chose to visit Montpellier because I thought it was also on the Mediterranean (my foolish mistake) and the city promotes itself as the second gayest city after Paris. I had rented an apartment for four weeks and thus, was stuck in a town that is really more appropriate for a long weekend visit. The apartment was a fifth floor walk-up so I tried to plan my days to minimize the stair climbing. I'll no longer do more than three stories! I was unable to find many gay people or bars or any gay venues and there isn't very much to do there in terms of sightseeing except to visit the old section of the city. During my stay there, I visited Arles in the hopes of visiting the haunts of Vincent van Gogh including the yellow house. To my surprise, there was virtually nothing in Arles about Vincent except for the sale of prints of his works. It turns out that the yellow house was destroyed by the Americans during World War II in the fight against the Nazis who were occupying France. I decided that I would use the phrase "24 hours in Arles" as a synonym for "boring."

One afternoon, while visiting a fabulous gelato shop in Montpellier, I tripped over a very thin curb and took another dramatic "tumble." Of course, I jumped up and hoped that not too many people witnessed my gracefulness. I thought I would be in a good deal of pain the next day but, fortunately, that was not the case. You just never know when the tumbling talent will come in handy.

I did find a lovely restaurant in Montpellier called Didaskali which was ranked #2 out of 551 restaurants by the website, TripAdvisor. The restaurant was tiny but the food was excellent and reasonably priced. I had a bowl of vegetable soup and a large salad with chicken and I have to say that the food was very good and very fresh. The owner Laurence (who is also the chief cook and bottle washer) is friendly, gracious, and very accommodating.

On another occasion, I went out to dinner at a café/restaurant in the central plaza area of Montpellier that specializes in mussels and French fries, which is a very popular dish in the south. I sat down at a table on the outdoor patio. The waiter comes by, hands me a menu and goes away. Upon his return, I ordered one of the entrées of mussels that sounded along with a quarter (liter) of white wine. There was no chitchat from the waiter and in about a minute, he brings my wine. By the time I take a few sips, another waiter brings my mussels and fries. I am a fan of good service but this was so fast I could only think that they wanted me in and out quickly even though there was no wait for tables. There was no sign of my waiter during my meal. In France, the tip is usually included in the bill, which can sometimes be a disincentive to being attentive. After my fill of mussels and fries, I rejoined my glass of wine. After a while, one of the waiters cleared the dishes, asked if I wanted dessert or coffee, I declined, he left. As the wine winds down, I am still unable to get the waiter's attention. I finally wave him down and a few minutes later the check arrives. I searched for him once again to pay as I don't like leaving money on an outside table. I finally gave the money to another waiter and I left. What struck me that night was the invisibility of the lone diner or maybe it was just the apathy of the waiter that emphasized the aloneness whereas the tiniest bit of small talk would have made the meal far more enjoyable. As I get older, it takes more work to eat dinner alone.

Both Nice and Montpellier are pleasant cities to visit for short respites but they are not what I would call cosmopolitan. It became quite clear from these side trips that, for me, Paris is France and vice versa.

La vie en rosé

The Paris gay area is the Marais. It is also the old, and still current, Jewish neighborhood. It is very upscale with all the high-end shops, trendy bars and restaurants and lots of gay men. I have visited the Marais many times through the years and I am pretty familiar with the area. There are many gay bars and restaurants, gay saunas, gay shops and bookstores in the Marais and the surrounding area. Several blocks from the Marais, near the Arts et Métiers metro stop, is the Paris LGBT Center, a resource for all things LGBT in the city. They also have complimentary Wi-Fi.

Bars and restaurants here are expensive and currently do not fit into my meager budget. Even at happy hour, a pint of draft beer costs about $8 or $9. Accordingly, my gay social life in Paris has been rather low-key. I have been to a couple of bars, the Bear's Den and Le Cox. Both bars have a somewhat older crowd (older than 30). I generally go to happy hours when I do go out and usually start talking to English speakers, if possible, because the bars are so small that the background noise makes it very difficult to hear and more exhausting to speak and understand French.

I joined a gay group called OutParis that I found on Meetup.com in an effort to start making gay friends. I've attended a few of their events met some nice people. I admit that I have been putting most of my energy into creative endeavors rather than social ones. Upon my next return I hope to pursue more activities in the gayer environments.

In June I attended my first Paris Gay Pride (Marche des Fiertés). The parade was a lot of fun despite light to heavy rain all day. People were celebrating same-sex marriage, which had recently been passed in France. There weren't too many floats or vendors, just lots and lots of people walking, dancing and frolicking along the parade route. I managed to watch the three-hour parade before returning to the dry warmth of my home.

Culture Rapide/Paris Lit Up

During my first month in Paris, I found an English-speaking open mic night sponsored by a literary group called Paris Lit Up and held every

Thursday night at a bar/performance space called Culture Rapide in the area of the city called Belleville. Anyone can read or perform on Thursdays just by signing up. There are usually two or three rounds of performances. In the states, an open mic usually hosts budding stand-up comics so I wrote a short, humorous piece about lawyers. I quickly found out that poets dominate the open mics here although all styles of writing and/or performance are welcome. Hence, my long-dormant stabs at poetry were resuscitated — when in poet-town one waxes poetic! It's actually quite fun for me because poetry doesn't have those nasty demands of capitalization, punctuation or even full sentences. Since short, satirical stories are my forte, I generally alternated between poems and stories.

The Thursday open mic creates an instant community. People are very friendly and welcoming. After two brief trips to DC, I was warmly greeted upon my return like a homecoming of sorts. There are some very talented poets, writers and singers who attend. They don't just write or sing. They sing, compose music, play several instruments, write poetry, novels and plays, create photos, videos and films, and try to keep their souls intact in the quest for artistic careers.

Many of the younger poets (under 30 years old) write about their emotional upheavals such as the lost true love, the onset of depression, or family difficulties. Some of the older poets (30 – 40 years old) take unique routes in their poetry: one writes poems about science fiction and Japanese anime; another reads bawdy poems in Latin followed by the English translations; a third writes humorous verse about CERN, the nuclear research center in Switzerland. And the rest of us (let's just say over 40) tend to write more about current political and religious issues. Each Thursday night presents a popular, perhaps peculiar, potpourri of poetic proficiency!

One night, at Culture Rapide, a Frenchman, Benoit, recognized me from the Downtown Cafe. I was at first quite flattered until I realized the reason he remembered me. One night at Downtown Café, a performer walked through the audience asking some questions and when she came to me I could only say that I didn't comprehend the question. A few chuckles rippled through the audience. As they say, there is no bad PR!

I got to be the guest host for one Thursday at Paris Lit Up! The lights above the stage are extremely hot and I was sweating a good deal. Between performers I made some jokes about sweating which morphed into bathhouses and saunas and keeping one's face and body young with steam. While reviews were mixed on my ad libbed comedy, I decided long ago that if people don't laugh at my jokes, it is no reflection on my sense of humor!

Paris Lit Up also publishes a literary magazine. This past September (2014) they launched their second edition in conjunction with a worldwide event called 100 Thousands Poets for Change. I intended to read two poems accompanied by a jazz quartet. The trombonist, however, was so loud that I had to scream into the microphone to hear myself talk. Due to time limits I was unable to read the second poem.

The following day, my six-month visa was to expire and I was off to DC for what I thought would be a mere two weeks stint before returning to Paris for an additional three months. Unfortunately, the two young men who were subletting my apartment and who were purportedly staying for the entire three months, snuck out with all their belongings the day before my return flight. The incident cost me a good deal of money to change my tickets, stay in DC for an additional three weeks, and lose three weeks of rent on my apartment in Paris. I can only hope there is such a thing as karma. I was quickly able to re-sublet the apartment for the desired amount of time and I was soon back in my new home city.

Downtown Café

I also attend a French-language open-mic at the Downtown Cafe, just four metro stops away. I figured I would never improve my French if I kept hanging out with the English speakers. The French open mic is held every Monday and is more of a poetry slam. My definition of slam poetry is rap without the music. The readers/performers at the Downtown Cafe speak so rapidly that I was only able to comprehend about 10% of the performances. I am now close to about 40% but I can still only pick up concepts from words and phrases rather than whole sentences. I imagine my blank stares are endearing to the other performers! In my defense, a lot of French slang is used which I have yet to learn. I speak what they refer to as "school" French. If I ever reach 80% comprehension, I will have become a Master of the French Language Universe. All types of writing are welcome. I usually recite a poem that I have written in French after having someone check my spelling and grammar. The audience is incredibly supportive and there is always much applause. They seemed to like the fact that an American can write and perform in their language. The level of talent is quite high among with all the young kids who can slam away at lightning speed.

It has been a little more difficult to meet people at the French open mic which I think is partially due to language, both my lack of fluency in French and their concerns about speaking English. The more I continued to attend, the friendlier the crowd got. One night during the break, I was speaking to Loki, a French slam poet. He was with his eight year-old daughter who had also gotten up and masterfully recited a piece by memory. During the second round, Loki and his daughter got up together and sang a song in English just for me!

Another great thing about the open mics is that I can sing without having to pay any money! I love to sing but I have a limited range and must be careful as to which songs I choose. Nonetheless, I have sung in both French and English at both venues albeit to very mixed reviews from "pleasant voice" to "terrible! I even sang a medley of show tunes in French. I love to sing and these opportunities may be my last chances to sing in public since Broadway has refused to return my calls for decades.

Montmartre Dionysia

There is a biannual festival competition of original one-act plays in English called the Montmartre Dionysia. Two writers, Albert Alla and Chris Newens, created the festival. The first play competition was staged in November 2013. Number two debuted in May 2014 and the third edition was held during the first week of December 2014. The plays are performed first in a very small theater in Montmartre called the Petit Théâtre du Bonheur (25-seat capacity). The final competition night is held on a boat, the Alternat, which is docked on the Seine and can accommodate close to 150 people.

I have the distinction of being one of the very few actors (if not the only one) to have performed in all three festivals! I acted in two separate one-acts plays, written and directed by Chris Newens, entitled "Tortoise" and "Mixed Freestyle Farce." This past December, I had a small role in a new one-act play entitled "Yellow Sable Coat," a comedy written and directed by Gina Cargas, a young woman from San Francisco. We were the "gay play" with two lesbians and myself.

In addition to the plays, there are several one-minute "anti-commercials" between acts. I have written and performed two of them creating new lyrics for popular melodies to satirize life in Paris. My first anti-commercial was entitled, "Lookin' For a Wife, I Am," to the retro tune of Herman's Hermits' "I'm Henry the Eighth I Am," and the second, "Paris, Paris," to the tune of "New York, New York." Following are the lyrics to the two song parodies.

Lookin' For a Wife, I Am

I'm lookin' for a wife, I am
Lookin' for a wife, I am, I am
She needn't be the girl next door
Just so long as she ain't a whore

For a bubble butt I'll scream hooray
A six-pack would be extraordin-ay
A bulge in the crotch would make me sway
But that'll wait for another day, cuz

I'm lookin' for a wife, I am
Lookin' for a wife, I am, I am
She needn't be the girl next door
Just so long as she ain't a whore

I promise there'll be no outlay
I'd say no way, to a bit of pay
And your legs I will not splay
Cuz in gay Paris I gotta stay, so

I'm lookin' for a wife, I am
Lookin' for a wife, I am, I am
She needn't be the girl next door
And I don't care if she is a whore!

<u>Paris, Paris</u>

Start spreading the brie, I'm kneading the dough
I want to baste a part of it, Paris, Paris

My copper saucepans, can't wait to flambé
Right to the Cordon Bleu of it, Paris, Paris.

I wanna bake it, in the city that doesn't deep - FRY
And find I'm king of the grill, a prime cut of beef, three Michelin stars!

These little town jams, so fruity and gay
I'll make a brand new tart of it in old Paris.

If I can BAKE it there, I'll bake it anywhere.
It's up to you, Paris, Paris!

These could become new shower-tune songs for all those tiring of the traditional musical theater medleys.

Crazy is as ...

I did have one particularly bizarre incident during my time in Paris. I was having some friends over for dinner and shortly before ten o'clock some guy starts yelling the window about the noise even though we were not being noisy at all. He moved the two plants and their stands away from my two windows as if he wanted to throw something through the window or perhaps come into the apartment. When I went outside, he tried to kick me in the groin, threatened to strangle me, and told me that he would send me to the hospital. He also called me a *pédé*, which is a pejorative for gay. One of my dinner guests who is fluent in French told me that he heard the man make several anti-gay comments regarding both my guests and myself. There was certainly a homophobic element to the situation. I called the police who came very quickly but the man had already left the courtyard. They told me to file a formal complaint with the police department in my district and to call immediately if anything else happened. They also told me that homophobic comments are a hate crime in France.

The following afternoon I put the plants and stands back where they belong. Moments later he was out the courtyard moving them again

28

and screaming things at me in incomprehensible French. I screamed back at him in English He then came over to my window and slammed the outside shutters in my face. I grabbed my passport, phone and money and went outside and called the police who, again, arrived in minutes. I went to the police station to file a formal complaint. One of the guys in the building, who lives below crazy guy, returned the plants and stands to their proper place in front of my windows, where they remain. He also verified that the guy is a "weekend" alcoholic. I have not seen crazy guy again.

Charlie Hebdo

On January 7, there were the brutal attacks and murders of the staff at the satiric newspaper, Charlie Hebdo and also at a kosher Jewish supermarket. Seventeen people were killed by a few Islamic jihadists. It was a horrific act that instilled fear in the citizens of Paris as well as anxiety about possible future attacks. Makeshift memorials popped up around the city and there were several vigils to commemorate the murder victims. On Sunday, January 11, there was a huge march from Place de la République to Place de la Nation. The crowd was guesstimated at over one million people. The usual half-hour or so walk between the two squares took more than five hours for large crowd to complete the march.

Chez-soi

I finished the manuscript for this book shortly before I left Paris on January 18. I returned to the States with sixty dollars to my name. However, not one cent was wasted on my time in Paris. For me, the time in Paris was truly like a rebirth, both artistically and, to use that nebulous term, spiritually. To bastardize the Buddhist cliché, whenever I'm in Paris, there I am! I look forward to a hasty return to my new home.

"There is in fact something obscene and sinister about photography, a desire to imprison, to incorporate, a sexual intensity of pursuit."
William S. Burroughs

JE SUIS UN APPAREIL-PHOTO 1

"The whole point of taking pictures is so that you don't have to explain things with words."
Elliott Erwitt

36

41

"I am assured by a very knowing American of my acquaintance in London, that a young healthy child, well nursed, is, at a year old, a most delicious, nourishing, and wholesome food."
Jonathan Swift

SATIRE IN PROSE

"I'd rather die standing than live on my knees."
Stéphane Charbonnier

44

Mixed Metaphors, or Optimism

Joe Candeed was a very successful businessman. His company, Plastic Joe, Inc., manufactured and sold special plastic ball bearings that significantly reduced friction and would last for fifty years. He frequently said to people, "My life is the best of all worlds," and "My balls run the world." Joe had owned the company for over 20 years and was a millionaire many times over. He loved to spend money. Joe owned elegant and spacious homes in New York, Beverly Hills and Paris. Joe was proud to say that nothing in his homes was energy efficient. He had a stable of twelve gas-guzzling cars including a Rolls Royce, a Maserati, and a Bentley. His art collection consisted of masterpieces from da Vinci and Rembrandt to Picasso and Dali. His wife, Scarlett, was bedecked by Tiffany's, Louis Vuitton and Chanel. Their two children, Joe, Jr. and Joan, attended the best private schools in Switzerland. The Candeed family lived in the best of all worlds.

Plastic Joe, Inc. was located in West Falia, New Jersey. Each morning Joe would take the train from Penn Station to West Falia. He wanted to give the impression that he was a regular Joe. Everyday, he would pass by Martin, a homeless man who regularly begged for money in front of Joe's office building. Once in a while, Joe would give Martin a quarter and say to him, "Three more and you can buy a cup of coffee. *Or*, you can just get a job!" Martin would accept the quarter while giving Joe the evil eye.

Joe's office was on the top floor of a building that had formerly housed a homeless shelter, a soup kitchen, and a clinic for drug addicts. When Joe bought the building, he terminated the leases of the non-profit organizations. His large office contained a wet bar, an espresso maker, a large-screen TV, and a full bathroom with a hot tub. He had autographed photos of Ayn Rand atop a marble fireplace. Joe had the best of all offices. Plastic Joe, Inc. had twenty employees who worked in the plant including a few illegal immigrants for whom Joe forged work papers. He paid them all the minimum wage with no benefits. Joe was living in the best of all worlds.

Joe's patent for his ball bearings had expired but he gave little thought to this as business had been booming for many years. One day, Joe read in the Wall Street Journal that several companies had sprung up using his formerly patented techniques to make similar plastic ball bearings. This did not faze him for Plastic Joe, Inc. was the leader in ball bearings. He said to himself, "My balls still run the world." The next day, Joe read that one of the companies, Baron's Bearings, Inc., was using Joe's ball bearings technology but with a patented, new and improved plastic. The new ball bearings further reduced friction, would last for a hundred years, and were cheaper to manufacture. The CEO, nicknamed "the Baron," was expanding the company daily. But Joe thought to himself, "His balls will never run the world."

Then tragedy struck. Baron's Bearings, Inc. overtook Plastic Joe, Inc. as the ball bearings leader. Joe started to panic as his stock dropped from $200 to $2 per share because all his wealth was tied to the company's stock. He was soon unable to pay the company bills and had to close down Plastic Joe, Inc. Upon hearing this news, Joe's wife, Scarlett, had a massive heart attack and died immediately. Joe, Jr. and Joan were detained in a Swiss prison for failure to pay tuition as a result of Joe's bounced checks.

Joe had little savings and was soon unable to make the huge payments on his mortgages and car loans. He was sure he could sell two of his mansions and several of his cars and be flush with money once again. However, a major recession caused by pandemonium in the stock market, scared off potential buyers. The bank foreclosed on Joe's homes and his cars were repossessed. In a New York minute, Joe found himself homeless. He had offended so many people over the years that he had no friends with whom to stay. Meanwhile, the employees of the now-shuttered Plastic Joe, Inc. were quickly able to secure jobs with the Baron at a higher pay, benefits and union membership.

Joe left his New York home with as many clothes and bed linens as he could carry. A few blocks from his former penthouse, he created the chicest makeshift tent and bed and settled in for his first night on the street. The next morning, as Joe sat on a designer pillow pondering his situation, he saw Martin who was dressed in a smart suit and carrying a briefcase. Joe thought he was imagining things. When Martin saw Joe, he just smiled and then explained that, out of the blue, he had inherited $50,000 from a very distant relative. He was able to clean up his drug habit, rent a studio apartment, and found a job with Baron's

Bearings, Inc. as an assistant in the accounting department. He then took twenty dollars out of his wallet, and gave it to Joe saying, "This should buy you some food and a couple bottles of cheap wine." As he was walking away, he turned and added, "Or, you can just get a job." Minutes later, a limousine stopped in front of Joe. The window rolled down and Joe could see that it was the Baron. The Baron looked at Joe, shook his head, and said, "Now *my* balls run the world," and drove off. Joe just muttered, "My life is the worst of all worlds." But, ever the optimist, he thought, tomorrow is another day and my balls will rise again.

Nightmare on Facebook

Ann was a big fan of Facebook. Everyday she would tell her friends about her life from the moment she got up until just before bedtime. She would post pictures of her dog, her little brother, family vacations and all her friends at school. She was so happy when people "like'd" what she posted because she wanted to be the most popular girl on Facebook. The best-looking senior at school, Jimmy Fuchs, invited Ann, who was only a sophomore, to the senior prom. As soon as she got home from the prom, Ann posted a selfie from her big night. She was so proud of the picture showing her new pink gown, her new hairdo, and most of all, the beautiful, jewel encrusted gold bracelet that Jimmy bought her just for the prom. Ann smiled as she admired her lovely new bracelet. She was the happiest girl in the world.

The following morning, Ann's best friends, Brenda, Marcy and Suzy, began to comment on the photo as posted in the following thread:

BRENDA:
Ann was so lucky to go to the prom with Jimmy.

MARCY:
I am soooooo jealous.

SUZY:
Look at that beautiful bracelet!

BRENDA:
It looks a little cheap to me. LOL

MARCY:
I think Jimmy made it from one of those costume jewelry kits!

SUZY:
LOL I think he bought it at Walmart.

BRENDA:
I heard he stole it from a homeless woman. LOL

MARCY:
That's strange. I just read about a homeless woman getting robbed.

SUZY:
OMG! Ann is wearing homeless jewelry! LOL

BRENDA:
LMAO Maybe Jimmy is really homeless and lives in an old beat-up car.

MARCY:
I'll bet Jimmy's mother is homeless, too, and he stole it from her.

SUZY:
Well, I've smelled b.o. on Jimmy. Maybe he can't afford soap or deodorant. LOL

BRENDA:
I heard his family is from Mississippi. They're all poor there.

MARCY:
I wonder if he smells when he's kissing Ann. LMAO

SUZY:
Ann had her nose fixed a couple of years ago and she might not be able to smell anything.

BRENDA:
LMAO You know she never said anything about the nose job to me but I thought something was different.

MARCY:
Well, she never talks about what her father does, either. She just says that he works for the government but who knows what that means.

SUZY:
I had a friend once whose father worked for the government and later we found out that he worked for the CIA.

BRENDA:
I wonder if we're being recorded when we go to her house? LOL

MARCY:
She does have all the latest smart products.

SUZY:
Maybe we should stay away from Ann and her family.

BRENDA:
I'm not sure but all this talk is making me nervous.

MARCY:
I think we better stay away from her until we find out more.

SUZY:
We can't take the chance we're being watched by the CIA every time we go to her house.

BRENDA:
So what are you guys wearing to school tomorrow?

MARCY:
I'm not sure yet. Let's meet at Starbucks in fifteen minutes and hang out.

SUZY:
See you there.

BRENDA:
Me, too.

When she awoke, Ann saw that she had notifications on Facebook. Her three best friends had "like'd" and commented on her photo. As she began to read the thread under her cherished photo she welled up, tears began to fall turning into sobs and finally into anguished weeping. After several minutes the tears subsided and a seething rage built up inside her. She would go to Starbucks and confront them. How could her three best friends be so mean? She passed through the kitchen and headed out the front door.

Starbucks was just a ten-minute walk from Ann's house. As she approached the coffee shop she could see her three best friends seated at a small table, laughing. The girls did not see Ann enter and as she approached the table, Brenda screamed while Marcy and Suzy sat dumbstruck. Brandishing a ten-inch carving knife, Ann stabbed each girl repeatedly until a river of blood covered the white, tiled floor. The baristas and the other patrons ran out, screaming. Ann, splattered with blood, grabbed a coffee, looked down at her three best friends and snarled, "Now I'm LMAO!"

Ann was tried as an adult and received three consecutive life sentences. She is currently incarcerated at a women's prison in rural Mississippi. Facebook amended its privacy policy with an option not to allow comments on posted photographs.

Bastille Day: A Half-Baked History

Jacques Valjacques was the sixteen year-old scion of a well-known family of tailors and seamstresses. He was the son of Rafe Lauren Valjacques, tailor to King Louis XVI. Jacques was a troublesome young man who did not get along with his stepmother, Bertie Roth Valjacques, who would later sew the original tricolor flag. After one too many "*Vas te faire foutre!*"s from Jacques, she insisted that Rafe throw him out of the house. During a boisterous confrontation, Rafe threw Jacques out of the house with a small satchel containing a hundred francs.

Being the smart ass that he was, he spent the money at the first brothel he found. He chose the buxom brunette, Sarah Putain, who had the reputation as the best whore in Paris. Unfortunately for Jacques, he had a problem with premature ejaculation, so his 100 francs only bought him a 10-minute session. He was then forced to live on the dusty streets of Paris. Two days went by and he was very hungry. He had to find something to eat. He went into a boulangerie and could smell the freshly baked baguettes. His mouth started to water as he stared at the chocolate croissants and the trays of beautiful pastries. The kindly *boulanger*, Monsieur Jules Enfant, asked Jacques what he would like. Jacques asked him if he had a freshly baked chocolate croissant with the chocolate all soft and gooey inside. The *boulanger* smiled and went into the kitchen to check. Jacques quickly grabbed an armful of baguettes and bolted out the door. He ran as fast as he could for about 500 meters until he reached the Bastille prison. When Chef Enfant returned from the kitchen and saw that Jacques had absconded with the baguettes, he immediately hailed the ace gendarme, Thomas Hilfiguerre, known for his trademark blue, white and red plaid beret. Gendarme Hilfiguerre quickly went off to find the young thief.

Jacques was familiar with the Bastille prison because his uncle, Hugo Patron Valjacques, had been jailed there when, as a young apprentice, he inadvertently sewed up the backside of King Louis XV's breeches causing the king to defecate in them. Imprisoned in the Bastille, Hugo was never seen again. Feeling safe, Jacques sat down against a wall of the Bastille and smoked a Gauloises. The cigarettes had just been introduced onto the market and were the first with an activated charcoal filter. Jacques was about to take his final drag when he spotted the famous red, white and blue beret. Panicking, he tossed his still lit cigarette over the 80 foot Bastille wall. (Jacques had been a pitcher for the Paris Peasants stickball team) and started running with Gendarme Hilfiguerre in hot pursuit. The lit cigarette landed on a keg of gunpowder on the other side of the prison wall. Suddenly, there was an enormous explosion, powerful enough to cause Jacques to fall to the ground. He could see Gendarme Hilfiguerre, engulfed in flames. The gendarme erupted into a fiery array of blue, white and red. These colors would later become a major theme of fireworks displayed in celebration of the day.

Jacques was dumbstruck as he watched the black clouds of smoke encircle the Bastille. Within moments, a crowd began to storm the prison. The commandant of the prison, Charles of Gaul, was soon seen in a parapet waving a white flag as the madding crowd stormed the fortress. Jacques watched fearfully as seven prisoners were dragged from the burning edifice. One of the prisoners looked oddly familiar. Could it be? *Non.* Could it be? *Oui!* It was old Uncle Hugo but he appeared quite different from what Jacques remembered. Jacques ran to his long-thought-dead uncle and embraced him. As he did so, he felt what he thought were breasts. And they were! Uncle Hugo explained that while in prison he realized that he was a woman trapped in a man's body and is now living as a woman with his new name, Vanille Chanel. She would later create the simple black peasant dress that would one day eradicate color in Paris fashion. They both burst into tears over this long-overdue reunion. Jacques brought her home to his father who was overjoyed to see his newfound brother or rather, his newfound sister. There was much joy and celebration in the Valjacques home that night. Jacques made nice with Bertie and moved back home.

Word soon got out that Jacques had started the explosion that demolished the Bastille. The people of Paris were elated and Jacques became a hero of the insurrection. A ticker-tape parade was held in his honor. There was talk of calling the day of independence "Valjacques Day" but since the royalists were still upset about the whole defecation incident, the name Bastille Day was chosen. The Parisians still smoke Gauloises today in tribute to Jacques' valor.

Jacques was the toast of Paris for years to come. He began an apprenticeship with Aunt Vanille and went on to create a very successful couture line under the brand name Yves Saint-Jacques. He fell in love with the prostitute, Sarah Putain. They married and had a large family of well-dressed and sexually active children.

Clean Conceptions

NEWS FLASH: The New York Times has reported that a rash of babies were born to teen-aged mothers during the winter solstice in New York City without any discernible fathers in sight. The fathers were neither absent, dead, or missing in action. According to an unofficial census, the estimated 666 offspring were conceived without any evidence of male sperm. Each of the women has declared, "Nobody ever did me! It's a friggin' miracle!" None of the New York inns had any available rooms because of all the holiday parties so a makeshift delivery room was fashioned from an empty Pottery Barn to accommodate the extraordinary amount of births. These babies have been born without any trace of a Y chromosome. Both male and female offspring appear to have the rare G-D chromosome that only occurs every 2000 years, designated as XXG-D in girls and XG-D in boys.

Doctors are baffled, perplexed and enigmatized. They have convened an emergency meeting of the Obstetrics/Gynecology subsection of the American Medical Association to investigate the phenomenon referred to as Clean Conception Syndrome or CCS. To add to the confusion, three drag kings from the Orient-R bar in the East Village accompanied by the east coast's brightest drag star, Rufus St. Paul, have visited the newborns. The drag kings have brought gifts of gold-toned bling, Old Spice, and licorice-scented potpourri, to all the new mothers. In a related incident, a gathering of farm animals including sheep, goats, cows, oxen, dogs, cats, squirrels, rats and 'possums, has appeared in front of the Pottery Barn. It is believed that they have all escaped from the Bronx Zoo. Meanwhile, in Central Park, an unprecedented assemblage of drummers has formed with such luminaries as Ringo Starr, Tommy Lee and Nick Jonas. Recordings of Paul Anka's "(You're) Having my Baby" and Stevie Wonder's "Isn't She Lovely" (amended to "Aren't They So Lovely") can be heard throughout the park like angelic choirs.

Pandemonium has broken out in the Upper East Side where society women have stormed hospitals and Pottery Barns, desperate to learn the secret of male-free conception. The mayor has issued a state of emergency and has called out the National Guard, the ASPCA and the two Glorias, Steinem and Allred. Planned Parenthood has shuttered its

New York City offices and right wing Christians, Jews and Muslims are accusing the women of blasphemy and being two-bit whores.

The newborns have been swaddled through the generosity of OshKosh B'Gosh and Pampers is donating free diapers for a year. Public Relations Agents have been retained by the women to holy ghostwrite personal memoirs and handle all commercial endorsements, public appearances, film rights, and the liposuction of excess baby fat. The mothers have already agreed to a reality television show entitled, "666 Miracles and Counting," to be hosted by the prolific Christian breeders, Michelle and Jim-Bob Duggar.

Due to the need for privacy and a spate of death threats, there will be an exodus of mothers and children to New Egypt, New Jersey, until January 6 when these magical babies will be baptized to preclude any trips to Limbo. Circumcision is optional.

In other pregnancy news, doctors in Arkansas have determined that Michelle Duggar, the aforementioned prolific birther, is the first woman in history not to go through menopause. Michelle claims that God appeared to her in a dream. He told her that her uterus was so stretched out, she could now only have multiple births. Since her nineteenth child, Michelle has given birth to a set of decatuplets or ten children at one time. She is the first woman known to have accomplished this feat and she has earned her place in the Guinness Book of World Records. Her reality show is now called *29 Kids and Incontinent*. Sadly, her husband Jim-Bob accidentally gave himself an irreparable vasectomy while chopping wood for the new nursery. This horrible accident notwithstanding, Michelle confessed she is very excited about her new role as spokesperson for Depends.

The Case of the Perrimasons

There is a well-known riddle that goes, "What do you call 10,000 lawyers chained together at the bottom of the ocean?" The answer is "A start!" I went to law school with the motivation that I would be able to wreak havoc on conservatives for their disdain and vitriol against gay people, people of color, and the poor. I quickly learned, however, that law school isn't really about the law. The "habeas secretus" of law school that was explained in great detail, will shock you. This educational enterprise is part of an intricate, all-encompassing battle plan. Each and every lawyer belongs to a secret society called "Skulls, Bones, Guts and Corpses" also known as the Loyal Order of Perrimasons. This secret society is the "one government" you've heard about that actually rules the world. It's the duplicitous scheme about which George Orwell tried to warn us.

Most people assume that lawyers cannot be trusted and that thinking like a lawyer is akin to having a criminal mind. They have no idea of the enormity of the conspiracy. Lawyers are running the whole game. According to the Congressional Yearly, almost 90% of the US Congressmen are lawyers (or JDs if unable to pass the bar). Under the guise of a constant logjam, Congress repeatedly confuses people into thinking that they care about the public welfare. This is nothing more than a dabbling in hyperbole. It's no accident that 26 out of the 43 men who served as president have been lawyers. While many of them have committed less-than-legal acts, they have been given the cover of "executive privilege." Only two of them have pissed off enough people that they were forced to perform in the one-act play entitled "Impeachment." The Supreme Court is resplendent with attorneys. It takes some pretty clever legalistic maneuvers to convince the public that a corporation is a person. The court regularly defends corporate America and the wealthy because they, too, belong to the infamous 1%. As a matter of fact, the majority of the 1% are attorneys plus a few people who are just really, really, really rich. This is how the Perrimasons are taking over the world.

The Roman Catholic Church is completely made up of lawyers but as a ruse they call themselves "canon" lawyers. The Catholic Church has been part of the global 1% for over a thousand years. BC and AC actually stand for before and after capitalism. Jesus was the original

CEO and is often referred to as an adherent of "the law." He bowdlerized his own sayings to create the Bible, the most profitable book of all time. It was originally called How to Get Rich and Influence Disciples but he felt that a shorter title would be easier to sell. Some of Jesus' actual proverbs were: "It is easier for a rich man to live like he's in heaven than it is to thread a needle," and "Store all your treasures under the bed because we haven't yet created the Fed." Originally, the golden rule was, "Do unto others before they do unto you." Marketing the book was easy since few could read at the time and therefore, the hoi polloi could be told pretty much anything about its contents. Jesus was the original Charles Ponzi. As a matter of fact, his last name, Christ, actually comes from the Aramaic word "koch" meaning pyramid scheme although when first coined, it actually referred to pyramids. Jesus created the model for all faith-based corporations since that time.

Despite a precarious reputation, the Perrimasons are experts in using various pretenses to acquire some measure of respect. The most popular one is to make lots and lots of money as corporate attorneys, tax attorneys, or highly paid defense attorneys and claim philanthropic acts. Some use politics to accomplish the same ends. Many work in firms, a code word for franchises. It is the firm that pays for any philanthropic endeavors. The huge incomes allow attorneys to control governments around the world. To confuse the skeptics and naysayers, approximately 0.001% of lawyers work in what they call Public Interest. These lawyers feign not to earn much money but they are actually bankrolled by the franchises. There is absolutely nothing anyone can do to curb this world takeover. The system is so entrenched in national and international affairs that it is impenetrable by the 99%. This cabal of lawyers is very excited by the rumors that Pope Francis will soon be eliminating the eighth commandment, the sin of lying. This will surely hasten the worldwide takeover strategy.

George Orwell once wrote, "I looked from man to pig and back again and I could see no difference." In the original manuscript of *Animal Farm*, all the dictatorial farm animals were lawyers but the publishers got nervous and they changed the wording to suggest Communists instead.

The multitude of lawyer jokes, including the riddle about 10,000 lawyers chained together at the bottom of the ocean, were made up by lawyers to fool the public into believing that the politicians actually run things. Even Shakespeare, when he scribbled that line about killing all the lawyers, was only a puppet in the grand scheme of the Perrimasons. Shakespeare didn't become famous because people were actually reading his works or attending the theatrical productions! He knew exactly where his butter was churned.

To my great surprise and profitability, law school turned out to be just like a magical courtroom drama where no lawyer ever loses a case. I gratefully thank the Loyal Order of the Perrimasons that I did not waste any time pursuing one of those plebian MFA degrees.

B-Boy

It was December 24 and the boy Jesus, of Nazareth, was about to turn thirteen and would soon be celebrating his bar mitzvah, the beginning of manhood. His parents, Joseph and Virgin Mary, were very excited about this birthday but Jesus was not happy. Ever since he told the boys at school that God was his real father, not Joseph, they started calling him bastard boy or b-boy, son of a V, and the almighty sperm. Everyday he would leave school in tears. Virgin Mary was worried sick about him but Jesus was too afraid to tell her the reason for his tears. Virgin Mary had her own problems as well. She had never had sex with Joseph as he found her to be a wanton woman. Her natural urges went unsatisfied. Jesus was angry with God for being an absentee father, having left the family after impregnating his mother. He hated Joseph for pretending to be his father while all of Nazareth suspected otherwise. The town gossip was unbearable. Jesus also despised carpentry and dreaded the idea of a career in the wooden arts. He decided to run away.

Just before midnight, Jesus crept out of the manger-style house. He was determined not to celebrate his birthday in this wretched place. After three days of travel, he reached the town of Cana, famous for its homemade wine. Jesus had not eaten in three days and was very hungry. As he wandered the streets of Cana, he came upon a boy about the same age who was munching on an unleavened baguette and drinking water from a silver flask. Jesus went over to him and said, "May I please have a bite of your unleavened baguette? I haven't eaten in three days and I am very hungry." The boy said, "Sure, but just a bite. This is my dinner." As Jesus looked at the boy, he saw a mirror image of himself. He was stupefied and exclaimed, "You look just like me. We could be twins. I'm Jesus of Nazareth. What are you called?" The boy replied, "I'm Moses but my family forbids mirrors in the house so I don't know what I look like. I guess I'll take your word for it." As Jesus bit into the unleavened baguette, five more baguettes suddenly appeared along with two small jars of caviar. "Wow, that was pretty cool!" said Moses. "Are you a magician or something?" In a stage whisper, Jesus retorted, "No, I just have these weird powers from my father's side of the family." Then Moses offered him the flask and Jesus greedily gulped down the water. When he returned the flask, Moses exclaimed, "The flask is still full even though you drank all the water." He took a sip. "Oh my God, it tastes like wine! Man, you are one cool dude. What brings you to Cana?" Jesus explained that he had run away from home so that he could become a man in a faraway place. Moses gave him a high five and said, "Man, I'd like to be in your family. Are they magic, too?" Jesus answered him saying, "Let's just say they are a little eccentric, bordering on the dysfunctional." After a few minutes, Moses said, "I have a great idea. Since we both look alike, let's switch families!" Jesus thought about this for a moment and with a big smile he agreed. "I'm in, just tell me where to go."

Moses and Jesus quickly made plans to switch families. Moses would go to Nazareth and live with Virgin Mary and Joseph while Jesus stayed in Cana with Moses' parents, Eve and Adam. Adam was the mayor of Cana and Eve chaired the wine-tasting committee. Jesus was excited. This was just what he needed. After several hours of exchanging notes, Moses prepared to leave. Jesus gave him the five unleavened baguettes and the caviar so he could eat along the way. Moses headed toward Nazareth and Jesus went off to the home of Eve and Adam. The two boys instinctively knew they would never see each other again.

Jesus trekked to the edge of town and, lo and behold, Moses' home was a large, converted inn with many rooms. As he entered the house, Eve said, "Moses, it's about time you got home. Now get to bed. It's a school night." (The Christmas holiday season had yet to be established.) Jesus quickly found Moses' bedroom. There was a king-sized bed and a set of Roman furniture but not a mirror in sight. No more straw beds for me, Jesus thought. In minutes he was sound asleep in the big bed with visions of sugarplums dancing in his head.

Meanwhile, Moses completed the three-day walk to Nazareth with a belly full of unleavened baguettes and caviar. When he reached Jesus' home, Virgin Mary and Joseph were jubilant. Six-day old birthday cake awaited him. Moses was taken aback when he saw the straw bed in which he was to sleep. What the hell, he thought, at least I'll learn some magic. The next day he began his apprenticeship in carpentry with Joseph. Unfortunately, Moses was somewhat clumsy and was unable to saw wood, hammer nails or assemble IKEA furniture. Exasperated, Joseph screamed, "Jesus Christ, if you don't get your act together, I'm going to crucify you!" Little did Moses know that this would be a harbinger of things to come.

As it came to pass, Jesus made many friends in Cana, thrived in school and went on to get an MBA in retailing — thanks to the unconditional love of Eve and Adam. Like Adam, Jesus went into politics and succeeded his stepdad as the mayor of Cana. During his tenure as mayor, Jesus was able to finagle a stock swap deal with the Cana Wine and Spirits Company, Ltd. He was quickly made CEO due to his ability to turn water into wine. He married Mary Magdalena who was from a good Canan family. They had twelve children, all boys, upon whom Adam and Eve doted shamelessly.

As it came to pass, Moses left the home of Virgin Mary and Joseph when he turned 30. He gave up carpentry and moved to Jerusalem without a single magic trick from Joseph. He tried to become a rabbi but his Hebrew skills were so poor that after three years he finally abandoned that career path. In desperation, he became a petty thief. One day, after he had stolen thirty silver pieces from the Iscariot family, he was caught and turned over to the Roman authorities. His punishment would be death by crucifixion. As his hands and feet were nailed to a tree. He screamed, "God, why have you forsaken me?" And a voice from the heavens replied, "You made your straw bed, so die in it." Moses expired and the heavens turned black and thunderous.

Jesus looked up at the sky and he knew that Moses was gone. His only thought was that it could have been he. The Cana Wine and Spirits Company thrived as Jesus continued turning water into wine. He added unleavened baguettes and caviar to the product line since it was just another wave of the hand for him. The production costs were minimal and profits soared. After forty years in the business Jesus transferred the company to his twelve sons.

As it came to pass, Jesus spent the remainder of his life in perfect harmony with the best wines at his disposal. As he lay on his deathbed, he told his family and friends, "I'll be back!" Because it was the Sabbath, he was buried very quickly in a makeshift tomb. Three days later, to the astonishment of his loved ones, Jesus appeared at the door of his home. He stayed for forty days. Word having spread about Jesus' comeback play from the dead, a large crowd gathered at the Sea of

Galilee where Jesus announced his return to God, his real father. He stepped into the sea planning to walk on it before ascending to the heavens but something went terribly awry. As he walked farther and farther into the sea expecting to rise above it, Jesus drowned. A wrathful voice sounded from above, "B-boys never go to heaven!"

The Church of J. Christ, Banker

Lloyd Blankfein (LB), the Chairman and CEO of Goldman Sachs (GS), was once described as a "vampire sucking the blood out of humanity." He is the soul of GS, the most famous investment bank in the world earning billions of dollars in profits each year. The only words to describe LB are "capitalist extraordinaire!" In his own words, this man, the essence of success, stated, "If I slit my wrists, people would cheer!"

It wasn't enough for LB to be number one. He wanted to make more money than any other investment bank would make in the next hundred years. One afternoon, after finishing a round of golf with John Boehner (JB), he was struck by an angelic calling. It was the angel Gabriel (AG) who had been promoted from birth announcements to financial revelations. Under a barrage of thunder, AG declared, "The Holy Father in heaven wants you to found a new religion, far greater than all others, to provide guidance for those who understand that money is the only supreme and eternal good. A shocked and awed LB looked at AG and queried, "Sure, but what's the catch? Is it wrong to make too much money... to have too much ambition... to be too successful?" AG replied, "Of course not. You must take care of your followers as you take care of yourself but without stock options. You are like an entrepreneurial shepherd watching over his flock." LB responded, "I don't want to put a cap on bonuses and limit their ambition. I believe God's work is already my own."

AG reassured him, saying, "It is through this spiritual endeavor, under your stewardship, that GS will become the most powerful investment bank in the world. Do you accept this divine business proposition?" "But what about all those biblical admonitions about making money, casting out the moneychangers, the whole eye of the camel thing, root of all evil, etc.?" LB asked. AG answered in a soothing voice, "Nothing but devious translations by the Catholics. They knew all too well that money was tantamount to love but they did not want to share the proceeds. So they lied and now I have to come to you, the Prophet of Prosperity (PP), to save the world from spiritual bankruptcy. We tried this once before with the Nobel laureate, L. Ron Hubbard (LRH), and Scientology but he pissed off the IRS so badly that his church became insolvent. Don't screw around with the IRS for their powers have yet to be fully understood." LB cried into the wilderness of Wall Street, "Who am I to turn down the Almighty Father. I am in this big time. Send me the business plan." AG replied, "There is no business plan. Create it as you will." Then he disappeared as quickly as he had arrived.

LB was so flabbergasted that he immediately made himself a drink of chilled Tequila Ley ($3.5 million per bottle) accompanied by a touch of Beluga caviar atop Perrier crackers. He was going to be the most successful investment banker ever. Take that, Jamie Dimon (JD)! He would create a new religion. It was brilliant. LB could barely believe that he did not think of this. GS would now be known as the First Church of J. Christ, Banker, a 501(c)(3) tax-exempt charitable organization to be listed as CJCB on the New York Stock Exchange (NYSE). He figured the J. Christ moniker would appeal to the Christians. LB would become the first CEO Supreme of the CJCB, comparable to the bishop of New York City. There would be no end to GS', or rather, CJCB's profits.

LB needed to come up with an organizational chart and some dogma. To keep it simple, there would be only two corporate commandments: 1) Money is the eternal good, and 2) Make more profit for yourself than you make for others. LB, as the CEO Supreme, would handle all financial matters including bonuses, "charitable" giving, and all donations from the congregation. The directors of the Federal Reserve Bank would become his College of Cardinals and the twelve Federal Reserve district banks would be his Quorum of the Twelve. There are no weekly services, no high or low holy days or any other stressful precepts. Plus, a complimentary subscription to the Wall Street Journal would be included with membership. The membership of the church will consist of all companies listed on the NYSE and NASDAQ, all investment banks and their subsidiaries, all other banks, and all current and former employees of the aforementioned companies. Tithing would be based on quarterly profits. Current MBA students are also eligible to join the church at a reduced rate. Members of the general public will be invited to join as soon as the church holds an initial public offering (IPO). There were rumors that Pope Francis would be nixing the eighth commandment prohibiting false witness. This new development would make CJCB immune to accusations of fraud and thereby increase the success of the IPO. Furthermore, the church will be legally designated as a person so that it may give unlimited funds to political candidates of both parties. LB was delirious with excitement!

This new church will be heralded as the most important milestone of American capitalism, the pièce de résistance for any investment banker. Thanks to AG, no other bank will have the same opportunity. Morgan Stanley, JP Morgan Chase, Merrill Lynch, and Citigroup can all eat dirt and go to hell! In a speech at LaGuardia Community College, in his role as CEO Supreme, LB uttered the profound and inspiring statement: "The Church of J. Christ, Banker, shall never fall far from heaven's gate."

A Movie Made in Heaven

It turns out that the creationists have been right all along. God spoke to me in a vivid dream and explained the big mystery. He actually did create the world in six days, as told in the Book of Genesis story, because heaven was so boring that He needed a good laugh. Adam and Eve really were the first two humans on earth. God said that it is far more fun to have all humans born from incestuous relationships. He wanted to be entertained by humans as long as possible.

God explained that for Him, human life is like an interactive Netflix solely for His entertainment. Human history is nothing more than a movie that He can fast forward, reverse or edit, depending on His mood.

During this incredible dialogue, I was permitted to ask God three questions. After a bit of contemplation, I came up with three questions that I felt would answer some of the great mysteries of the universe.

1. Who are Your favorite humans?

> I would have to say politicians because they are able to manipulate others, almost as well as I, using the whole gamut of emotions to persuade large numbers of people that they actually care about them. When I say politicians, I am also including all the religious leaders, as they are often able to stay one step ahead of the politicians in the accumulation of power, wealth and control. I am in absolute hysterics when I watch the meanderings of these master criminals. I am in awe of Myself as well for having created such self-centered and devious freaks.

> As to individuals, My favorites change from day to day. At the moment, I think I would say that My current favorites are Whoopi Goldberg and Paul Lynde. I don't mean to sound too retro but I just happened to recently catch the movie *Ghost* and a few episodes of *Bewitched* and the old *Hollywood Squares*. Have you seen *Ghost*? Whoopi was hysterical. I'm glad I gave her that Oscar. And who could be campier than Paul Lynde? He was the best center square, bar none. Two of

My consistent favorites are Judy Garland and Mother Theresa. I mean, c'mon, how can you not love Dorothy? She knew all along that she was a gay icon. You'd have to live in a cave not to get that whole "friend of Dorothy" thing. And Mother Theresa, now there was a real piece of work. She was just cunning and conniving enough to come out on top as selfless, holy, and revered. It's not easy to become a saint. It takes a lot of work, a lot of planning, and a lot of life-story revisions. You know, I also like that new guy, John Oliver, who rants about current injustices in a comical and yet pointed fashion. I'm not sure what he's going to do with his "free will" or, as I call it, editing, but he's got potential. Give me question number two.

2. Is the Bible actually the Word of You?

This is a good story. About 4000 years ago, some of the younger Israelites asked the elders to explain the meaning of life. Since many of the ancient civilizations had treated them shabbily, the elders decided to go with a one-god storyline rather than the more common and beloved multiple gods scheme. Now the elders had no idea what to say so they just made up stories to placate the young people. I mean, toilets, electricity and television had yet to be invented. Around the world people were defecating in their backyards and thinking the world might end when night fell. They knew nothing about the workings of the "universe," so I would provided them with opiates, marijuana and sometimes crack, and then I whispered in their ears the most outrageous lies I could think of without bursting with laughter. Since few people could read or write, these stories evolved orally — similar to the children's game of Telephone — with complex and contradictory characters and events until I thought that it should all be written down. I knew full well that the Catholic monks and priests would edit it later.

Some of the stories are true but most have been fabricated from the seeds of false witness that I had planted long ago. For example, Abraham and Moses were my great special effects guys. Can you imagine that I would tell Abraham to kill his own son or knock up an old lady or cut off the foreskin of all the males? For Christ's sake, I specifically made the foreskin to enhance the respite of pleasure that I thought sex would provide, a little break from evildoing.

Moses was a good actor. Do you think I would actually talk through a burning bush? That's a job for an amateur. *He* created the Ten Commandments to stop the wandering Israelites from screwing around so much. They were lost, bored, delirious from the heat, and driving each other crazy. They got a little rambunctious. I didn't stop Moses from reaching their promised land. He was an old man, completely exhausted, and he just died. I might have played that one better but I was watching the Egyptians build more pyramids and I lost track of some footage.

The whole Jesus story would take too much time but he perfected the model for religious scams. For the record, Jesus was not My son. What kind of Father would I be to kill my own son? Joseph was the one who knocked up Mary and was forced into a stone-thrown wedding by her father.

Mohammed gave Me a lot of laughs. He wasn't a very bright guy and with a few carefully chosen hallucinogens, I had him seeing crazy visions about world dominion and sadistic fantasies with seventy-two virgins coupled with a dash of pedophilia. He went out to conquer anybody and everybody, convincing tribe after tribe that he was My final and greatest prophet while amassing a slew of wives and concubines. Like many actors today, he wasn't an intellectual but he could put on a fabulous show full of sex and violence. I think you get the drift, so on to the last question.

3. Why do You allow wars, famine, disease, and all the other miseries of life?

The answer to that is a bit more complicated, kinda like a mystery/thriller novel. As you might suspect, I made good and evil two sides of the same coin. I needed to spice things up. Genocide, wars, famines, droughts, life-threatening diseases and disastrous weather created intriguing shows of hypocrisy, greed and arrogance that I never expected. I thought that some people would actually try to solve or prevent these calamities but I was wrong.

Just look at the right-wing Christians. They are far more interested and fascinated by gay sex rather than feeding the hungry or housing the homeless. For Me, it was like those documentaries that reveal the corruption of governments, banks and big business while convincing the masses that they did it all for their benefit. I deserve an Oscar for the best movie of all time. Plus, if everything was nice and rosy all the time I would be just as bored as I am with those choirs of angels singing off-key all day long.

Well, I feel much better having confessed so many of My secrets to you. But like any dream, you'll forget all of this within a couple of days. And FYI, no confessions are sacred. None of you can keep a secret for very long. I can't take the chance that you'll rat on Me and possibly destroy My game. Besides, they would put you away for coming up with such a crazy story. I'm going on vacation to hell next week. It's my version of Las Vegas and it's a long flight so I need some funny DVDs.

Have a nice life! As you have probably heard, it'll be over in the blink of eye — My eye!

I have recorded as much of this miraculous interview as possible. Despite my inability to remember story of creation for very long, I did get the last laugh. I traded my soul to Lucifer in exchange for the destruction of God's DVD player. It'll be a long flight to hell for Him!

An All Hallowed Eve's Carol

President Barack Obama had settled in for autumn night's sleep. The following day was Halloween and the First Lady had ordered him to pass out the candy to all the White House trick-or-treaters. His only other option was to spend the whole evening with Vice President Biden. It was a choice of two evils but at least there would be candy at the White House.

The President quickly dozed off but he was soon awoken by the sound of clanking metal. He jumped out of bed fearing the worst. To his amazement he espied Nancy Reagan in a black leather pantsuit and wrapped in heavy, 18-karat gold-plated chains. Suddenly she bellowed, "I am the ghost of Republicans past and I am here to show you what you have created so far." They walked out to the Truman Balcony and the President could see Yemen in the distance. Drones were hovering high above the hijab-covered country and random bodies were flying through the air. "This is what has pissed off the jihadists," Nancy screamed in a shrewish voice. The President begged Nancy to stop but she retorted, "Just one more thing, you have increased the budget so much that the national debt will be your legacy, surpassing even the wild spending of my Ronnie. You best solve daily crossword puzzles or you, too, will become senile before your second term ends." He covered his face in horror and screamed, "No more, no more!" Nancy started to fade away which was not difficult, as she weighed only 73 pounds. Before disappearing, she warned him, "My astrologer says that you will be visited by two more apparitions before the night is over." And with a few final clanks, she was gone.

Barack jumped into bed and hid under the covers. In a loud whisper, he prayed, "Allah, why have you forsaken me?" Just then he heard the sound of a gunshot and a cranky voice saying, "Damn, I shot him again!" The President peeled the covers from his face and there was Dick Cheney, gun in hand and wearing a tee shirt that read, "Friends - you can't live with them but you can shoot them." Then, in a ghoulish voice, he declared, "I am the ghost of Republicans present and I am here to show you the mistakes that I fraudulently accuse you of." Barack quickly admonished him saying, "I knew you would end a sentence with a preposition." Cheney took the president out to the Truman Balcony and suddenly there appeared the Rev. Jeremiah

Wright holding a Kenyan birth certificate. Cheney continued in a menacingly authoritative voice, "We, the birthers, know that you were not born in Hawaii and that you are a radical Muslim." With gun residue still on his hands, he started to fade while giving the President a final warning. "You will be visited by one more republican ghost before the night is over. Resign now before we, the Christians, impeach you for not being a real American." And he vanished from sight.

Barack jumped into bed once more, trembling, and screamed, "Allah, please take this cup from me." Before he could say anymore, Sarah Palin, in a moose skin jacket and skirt, appeared before him, exclaiming, "I am the ghost of Republicans future." Barack let out a hearty laugh and said, "Oh please, you think you can see Russia from your window. You have no political future." Palin snapped back saying, "Due to your popularity figures, I'm starting to look real good." She then took the President out to the Truman Balcony, which was starting to sag after all the night's activity. Suddenly, there appeared an ominous cloud hovering over rising oceans and flooded coastlines. School textbooks entitled "Creationism" in gothic script were dropping from the cloud like drones on the city of Washington. He let out a bloodcurdling scream as he watched Sarah grow faint. Before she dissolved, she uttered in a serious voice, "I see Russia everyday and Putin doesn't read the New York Times either." She then disappeared into the ominous cloud.

The shaken President jumped into bed and quickly fell asleep. In what seemed like minutes, he awoke with the sun streaming brightly into the Lincoln bedroom. This time the President jumped *out* of bed realizing he still had time to avert a Palin presidency. He sold all the White House furnishings including the Nancy Reagan china and leftover copies of his books, ended the drone attacks on Yemen and other Muslim countries and ordered the military to drop baby drones on all the congressional offices. The national debt plummeted within hours. The government saved enough money to create the largest surplus since Bill Clinton. In a final gesture, he had Putin's KGB kidnap Sarah Palin and bring her to Siberia until after the 2016 elections.

As he passed out candy to the little children that Halloween night, the President exclaimed, "Allah, bless us all, everyone!"

Saints and Snakes of the Emerald Isle

According to legend, St. Patrick, the patron saint of the Emerald Isle of Ireland, banished all the snakes from the country, chasing them into the sea after they attacked him during a forty-day fast. The true story, however, is of a far more depraved forty-hour period and has been hidden from history for over sixteen centuries. But one glorious Easter morn stacks of gilded and emerald-encrusted papyrus documents were resurrected under the famed Blarney Stone. The Irish government immediately put the documents under lock and key fearing another Easter uprising. After much thought about the upcoming elections, the government relented and released the documents the following year on March 17, the anniversary of the death of the popular saint. The Irish public embraced the story like a dazzling green gemstone and the blarney was no more.

Patrick was born in Roman Britain and at the age of sixteen he was kidnapped by a group of Irish pirates and brought to Ireland as a slave. He had to work as a lowly shepherd in County Antrim spending his days in spiritual contemplation and masturbation. As time passed, Patrick met a young woman named Brigit who, unbeknownst to Patrick, was a pagan goddess. Every afternoon Brigit came to see Patrick and they talked for hours. She had strawberry-blonde hair that shone in the sun, emerald eyes that danced when she smiled, and the requisite Irish freckles. Patrick fell madly in love with her. He was consumed with both love and lust. Brigit knew she had him under her spell. Late one afternoon, she took Patrick to a nearby cave that she called the Emerald City. Deep inside they came to a large stone altar covered with four-leaf shamrocks. Brigit lay down on the altar and motioned for Patrick to get on top of her. He began to kiss her entire body and as he did so, he was carried away in a tornado of lust. They made passionate love during forty hours of debauchery and then fell asleep side by side.

Brigit was gone when Patrick awoke. He started to panic wondering if it had all been a dream. He then heard a shrill, piercing laugh and when he looked up there was Brigit but instead of her strawberry-blond hair there were snakes surrounding her head and her emerald eyes had dissolved into a hideous, goblin-green face before him. She screamed, "I am the granddaughter of Medusa and I am going to have your child!" Patrick knew that if he looked directly at her, he would turn to stone, so he ran out of the cave and kept running until he reached the emerald-green sea. Brigit chased him, gliding on the air above. Patrick started to swim away as Brigit swooped down to attack him. She didn't know that the water would cause her to melt away (a common cause of death for wicked, green-faced goddesses). Patrick grabbed her and held her under the emerald-green water until she ceased to move and began to dissipate. He saw the snakes slither from her head and vanish out to sea, to be seen no more.

Patrick returned to shore, exhausted, and as he rested, the Brigit he knew with the strawberry-blond hair and the emerald eyes rose from the sea and walked toward him like a virgin aglow in an emerald-green aura. But Patrick now feared and despised her and her sex. He screamed at her that he would never have sex with a woman again and ran to the first monastery he could find. He knew he would be safe and there would be no chance of sex with a woman. He prayed and ate boiled corned beef and cabbage. He prayed and made Irish cream whiskey. He prayed and sang "Danny Boy." He prayed the Old Irish Blessing but the road did not rise up to meet him and he died on March 17, 493. He watched the Lord descend on an emerald-green cloud to greet him. Shortly thereafter, he was made a saint and that is the story of how St. Patrick chased the snakes out of the Emerald Isle and established his place in Irish history.

Meanwhile, Brigit was devastated by Patrick's rejection and she became a prostitute for the Irish pirates, calling herself "the Emerald Kitten." As she aged and lost her looks, she was shunned from the pirate world and spent the rest of her days in a nunnery until she died from what we now know as syphilis. As her mind deteriorated, she thought she saw St. Patrick and the Lord descending on an emerald-green cloud but she was insane and finally died circa 524. The legend of St. Patrick and the snakes was born only to be adulterated throughout years of oral tradition. For her sacrifice, Brigit became the junior saint of Ireland and patron of syphilitics. This is why the Irish men drink so much on St. Patrick's Day. They can't take the chance of looking the women they pick up in the eye and turning to stone. Similarly, the Irish women feed the men enough drinks to pass out, thus avoiding both sex and syphilis.

N.B. In another ironic twist, Brigit did give birth to her love child with St. Patrick. She called the child Osgar the Wild who turned out to be the ancestor of a famous Irish writer.

Boatloads

Mark Tyne and Val Hall were the best of friends. They were roommates living on a houseboat on the Missouri River in Kansas City, Missouri. One might even say that their relationship was a "bromance." While they each had steady girlfriends, they preferred hanging out with each other. It was 1918 and on November 11, the War to End All Wars was finally over. Mark and Val had been too young to go to war but they had high hopes for 1919, the new year of peace. They decided to start a business together to become rich and famous. In the weeks following the armistice, soldiers were returning home by the boatloads, literally. Appreciative women mobbed the returning heroes in every city and town. Lightning suddenly struck Mark and Val. They had to take advantage of all the new romances that were burgeoning throughout the state. They could make boatloads of money, literally, on romantic love that would certainly continue long after the veterans' return.

All they needed was a plan to make romance profitable year after year. They would have to do some research and who better to know about romance than their girlfriends, Ethel and Lucy. The women thought there should be a special day to celebrate romance with gifts from the men expressing their love and fidelity. They suggested February as the perfect month because men love to cuddle during the cold winter. The boys had visions of fame and boatloads of money, literally.

Mark and Val knew they had to create a yearly holiday to celebrate love and romance. They initially chose August 1 as the day since August was such a boring, hot, and sweaty month. But since air conditioning had yet to be invented, they thought, perhaps, the girls were right about February. It was a quiet month after the hubbub of Christmas and before the Easter holiday. February it would be but what should the holiday be called? Now it just so happened that Mark had a large collection of historical erotica that had cost him boatloads of money, figuratively. He had recently read about Cupid, the Roman god of desire and erotic love. He suggested the name, "Cupid's Day," to Val, adding "and you are my Cupid!" But Val didn't like the sound of Cupid's Day for he feared it would soon be called "Stupid's Day" since men would be forced to spend boatloads of money, figuratively, on gifts for the women. Val's eyes suddenly lit up. "Let's give our holiday a made-up name using some version of our own names." So they made a list of possible names. A famous name might be easier to market. Maybe, someone whose name was Mark or Val. They made a list: Mark Twain's Day, Val Kilmer's Day, Jean Val-jean's Day, Valtaire's Day, Karl Marks Day, the Marks Brothers' Day, Tyne Daly's Day, Hall and Oats' Day. None of these names sounded quite right. Maybe they should just use their own names. Mark-and-Val's Day? Val-and-Mark's Day? It still didn't sound right. Mark-and-Hall's Day? Hall-and-Tyne's Day? Val-and-Tyne's Day? That was it! VAL-AND-TYNE'S DAY! It was easy to pronounce and rolled off the tongue.

Now they had to decide on a date. The month would be February. Mark and Val had met when they were fourteen. Voila! February 14 became the date for Val-and-Tyne's Day. The final task was to create an easy gift for the men to give. Chocolates were messy and fattening. Flowers died quickly. Clothes and jewelry were too expensive. Val and Mark's eyes lit up at the same time and they simultaneously shouted "Greeting Cards!"

The cards would be cheap and easy to manufacture. The boys could make boatloads of money, literally. It was pure genius. Then Mark announced, "I've got the perfect name for our company – Markhall Cards." Val thought for a second and said, "How about Hallmark, like a stamp of purity." And that's how the Hallmark Greeting Card Company came to be. They still needed some seed money to get the business started. They went to see F.W. Woolworth of the five-and-dime stores. F.W. was very excited at the prospect and he offered them free office space and manufacturing costs in exchange for the rights to sell Hallmark Cards in his stores. Mark and Val were officially in business. They put ads in all the newspapers along the Missouri River. They sold so many greeting cards for the first Val-and-Tyne's Day that they actually made boatloads of money, literally.

This was the beginning of the Hallmark holiday we still celebrate all these years later. Sadly, Mark and Val were not able to enjoy the fruits of their labors for very long. On the second Val-and-Tyne's Day, in 1920, Ethel and Lucy found them in bed together and bludgeoned them to death, literally.

Vat's in a Name?

The National Security Agency (NSA) is having a public relations nightmare. Secrets have been leaked, whistleblowers are coming out en masse, surveillance programs have been uncovered, Verizon's stock is threatened, and the American citizenry is disgusted with the constant invasions of privacy. The NSA has turned to Henry Kissinger, an old friend, former club member, and architect of Richard Nixon's rise and fall, to advise the troubled agency. Long thought to be dead, the former National Security Advisor and Secretary of State has recommended two major changes in the organization: 1) a name change, and 2) a change in the mission statement.

The NSA directors at first balked at the suggested changes. Kissinger responded, "Look, I vuz down on my knees praying vith Richard Nixon and asking the Almighty Vahther to take this poison-villed cup vrom him. Unvortunately vah the President, He did not. After vee vaved good-bye to Dick as he boarded the plane back to California, I remained in power until that pansy Jimmy Carter came to town. Not vun president makes a move until he checks vith me. I know vaht I'm talking about. Espionage, invasion of privacy, deception, and verld domination are my fields of expertise. I understand vrom my sources that the Pope vill nix the commandment against false witness. This vill make all of our verk kosher. I didn't veecome Secretary of State because of my looks." The directors knew there was no question about that and they quickly took Kissinger's advice.

The NSA Directors, abetted by representatives from Google, Verizon, and Dick Cheney, chose a kindler, gentler name. The organization will now be known as the Security and Trust Alliance Network (SATAN). Kissinger felt that the new name would re-establish a façade of heartfelt commitment to the welfare of the American people. To give further evidence of their compassion, SATAN promised not to execute Ed Snowden should he ever return to the US until they decided otherwise. Kissinger also revealed plans for three new television shows entitled SATAN: New York, SATAN: DC, and SATAN: Miami. Comcast/NBC, who has long been a silent partner with SATAN, will produce the shows. He felt that television was the most efficient way to manipulate the American public. A feature film is in the works at 20th Century Fox under the direction of Rupert

Murdoch. Kissinger and Murdoch have been naked dance partners at the annual retreat of the elite, all-male, Bohemian Grove Club for over twenty years. All proceeds from the film and television series will go the top-secret SATAN black budget to cover all public relations costs associated with the new branding.

In a subsequent government poll, 63% of Americans did not know what the initials NSA stood for but were in favor of the new name, 21% were opposed, 4% did not understand the question, and 11% did not know who Kissinger was but were in favor of legalizing marijuana.

The mission statement of the SATAN was changed from:

> The National Security Agency leads the US Government in cryptology products and services in order to gain a decisive advantage for the Nation and our allies under all circumstances.

To the simpler:

> The SATAN is hell-bent to ensure your safety and security.

In a follow-up poll 63% did not know what a mission statement was, 21% thought the new statement was easier to understand, 4% did not understand the question, and 12% thought it was a cult but were in favor of legalizing marijuana.

So, in a very short period of time, thanks to the cunning of Dr. Kissinger, the NSA has transformed from a scandal-plagued operation to one of the most respected government agencies while maintaining all its invasive policies and programs. The public is delighted with integrity of the SATAN. To quote the late President Ronald Reagan, "A rose is a rose is a rose, until it isn't. This is what makes America great!"

Forever Noir

I landed in Paris with much excitement. It was New Year's Day, 1977. I had not been to Paris in over ten years. I hopped on the RER and before I knew it, I was in the center bulb of the city of lights. But alas, something was wrong. Everyone appeared to be in mourning. Who had died? Bardot? Foucault? St. Laurent? Who could have passed into the great beyond that would cause citizens of the fashion capital to dress in widow's weeds? Everyone, far and wide, was dressed in black. I started to ask passers-by, "Qui est mort? Each one looked at me like I was another crazy American tourist. I received no answer. I thought perhaps they didn't understand my French and yet, it was such a simple question. I rambled through the streets of Paris and could find no indication of any dead celebrity. No one was in tears, sad or despondent. Children were laughing and all seemed to be going about their daily business. I was completely frazzled. Finally, I asked a young man why everyone was wearing black. He looked at me like I had ten heads and declared, "C'est la mode!" I was speechless. Around the world fashion had moved forward. There were slogans like "purple is the new black," "red is the new black," "chartreuse is the new black." But in Paris, black was still the new black. It was incomprehensible!

I wandered aimlessly around the city until I found myself on the Champs-Elysées with the high-end shops and the fashionistas. Gazing in the windows, all I could see was one black outfit after another. The ubiquity was so dizzying I feared I would pass out. As I walked along a side street by the McDonald's, I suddenly heard the most harrowing, bloodcurdling scream. It was coming from the basement apartment directly in front of me. I peeked in but it was dark. The screams continued. I had to do something. A large, wooden, seventeenth century door was a few centimeters ajar. Using every ounce of strength I had, I was able to pry it open wide enough to squeeze my slender body into the dark cellar. The screams were coming from a Mlle. Defarge, an unemployed, homeless fashion writer who appeared to be a squatter in this dank cellar. Her face was ghostly white. As soon as she saw me, she babbled something in unintelligible French and bolted out the door in her black culottes and matching top. With my trusty BIC lighter I slowly walked forward until I came to an extremely narrow and winding set of stairs that seemed to lead to a secret cellar beneath the cellar. Garnering all my courage, I slowly maneuvered down the narrow, winding stairs. To my surprise, I found a fully equipped dungeon with leather chaps, handcuffs, whips, and jars of Crisco neatly arranged on cobwebbed shelves. I still could see no one but I could hear faint whimpers. As I forged ahead, I came to a solid steel door. I tried to open the door but my efforts were in vain. Fortuitously, I came upon a couple of day-old baguettes. Using the hardened bread as ramrods, I was able to push the door open just enough to squeeze my slender body into the pitch black room. With BIC lighter in hand, I slowly ventured forward. To my amazement, there were two incredibly wrinkled bodies, one male, and one female, shackled to the walls, emaciated, eyes closed and yet a faint wisp of air could be seen coming from their mouths due to the cold temperature of the room. I think they were relieved to hear me enter but, in their exhausted state, they could barely form a smile. Despite their forlorn appearances, there was something familiar about them. The woman had on what appeared to be a simple, terribly faded, black dress while the gentleman sported a faded pink sports jacket with faded and frayed black slacks. Upon opening her eyes just a sliver and gazing upon me, the woman slowly whispered the words, "cocoa, cocoa, cocoa." My first thought was that she wanted some chocolate. She then took a boney finger and pointed toward herself saying, "cocoa, cocoa, cocoa." I was mystified. As I stared at her and the faded black dress, I suddenly realized that she was saying, "Coco, Coco, Coco." It was Coco Chanel! Then she uttered the words, "crispy, crispy, crispy," and appeared to motion toward the old man. I looked again at the old man and, lo and behold, it was a wrinkled and shriveled version of Christian Dior! Her last words were "couleur, couleur, couleur." She then expired. I moved closer to the body and could see a wrinkled tattoo on her back just below the shoulder. It was a swastika. In a moment of delirious optimism, I hoped she was a devout Buddhist sporting the ancient symbol representing eternity. But with the probability that I was 99.9% wrong and having Jewish ancestors in my bloodline, I gave the motionless body several strong, swift kicks. I could hear her old, fragile bones snapping like popcorn in a microwave. The loud crunching of bones caused Dior to become more animated.

Now, as far as I knew, Christian Dior had died in 1957 after a strenuous sexual encounter and Coco had become a recluse living in Switzerland for many years and died in a Swiss mental hospital one year ago. I rushed upstairs and found a few more stale baguettes and some Orangina to give to Christian. He began to revive and was soon able to speak. He told me the story of their imprisonment. He and Coco had both planned brightly colored couture lines for 1957 in an effort to expand their customer base. When word of this got out, the French Council of Fashion was infuriated. They kidnapped the designers and brought them to this dark cellar. At the beginning they were treated kindly with regular meals and a subscription to the French edition of Vogue. During their initial confinement, Dior and Coco had a very short, dispassionate sexual relationship until his homosexual desires rendered him impotent. After a few years, they were only allowed day-old baguettes and flat Perrier and the subscription to Vogue had lapsed. The Fashion Council announced that Dior had perished in a boating accident on the Mediterranean and the body was never found. A memorial service was held and the House of Dior continued without him, introducing black, colorless couture lines each year. The Council attempted to put Coco on trial for her colorful treason but they were unable to find enough substantial evidence. So, in 1971, they simply declared that Coco had died in a psychiatric hospital in Switzerland, her body cremated and the ashes dispersed in the Swiss Alps. Coco and Chris remained in the dark, damp cellar until I stumbled upon them.

The Parisians were shocked when news of Dior's release became public. Chris was able to return to his fashion house with the understanding that all new designs would be black, gray or navy blue. Unfortunately, he would soon die from blood loss after severing his hand on a new, automatic, Singer sewing machine.

I quickly snuck out of Paris in my blasphemous baby blue seersucker suit. I knew now that it was the all-powerful Fashion Council who demanded that Parisians wear only black. I returned to Paris for one last time in 2013 and the Parisians were still wearing black. Of course, the benefit of a black ensemble is that you can wear the same outfit everyday, clean or not, and no one will notice. The only colors to be found in Paris were in the ubiquitous scarves that were the sole exemption authorized by the Council. Black had not come back for it had never left.

For the Love of God

Many Jews, Christians, and Muslims have long embraced the biblical admonitions requiring that "You shall not lie with a male as one lies with a female" and "You shall not have intercourse with any animal to be defiled with it." Having been deeply shamed by accusations of hypocrisy, the World Council of Sacred Teachings has instructed all Christian churches, Jewish synagogues and Muslim mosques to formalize additional admonitions from the sacred book of Leviticus regarding slavery and strict sexual mores. These rules and regulations are according to the word of God as handed down to Moses and recorded in the Torah, the Old Testament, and Islamic texts. Herewith, are the actual reinstated sacred demands from the all-powerful and all-loving God, Yahweh, Allah, as announced today in a joint press release.

1. You must not keep a slave's money until the morning.

2. A slave girl belongs to a man. Another man must not have sex with her for the girl is not free. He has not bought her. You must punish them. But you must not kill them because the girl was not free.

3. If an Israelite becomes poor, he might sell himself to another person. He must not work as a slave for that person. He must be like a paid servant.

4. Israel's people can buy male and female slaves. Those slaves must come from other countries and may have children who were born in your country. You can buy them.

5. If a man has sex with another man's wife you must kill him and the woman.

6. A man is sinning if he has sex with his father's wife. You must kill them both.

7. A man is sinning if he has sex with his son's wife. You must kill them both.

8. A man is sinning if he marries a woman and her mother. You must

burn the man and both the women in the fire.

9. A man must not have sex with a woman when she is bleeding. If he does, it is a sin. The people must send them away.

10. A man is unclean if he has sex with his aunt or his brother's wife. They will have no children.

The World Council of Sacred Teachings felt that they should add a couple admonitions from the Koran so as not to suffer the wrath of the Most High for the sin of religious discrimination. The Jews and the Christians thought that Islam was nothing more than a make-believe religion but they feared reprisals from the burgeoning, psychopathic Muslim jihadists, so they included the following:

"Modest dressing for all women is to be defined as covering everything except the face and hands in public. However, a veil is not compulsory in front of blind, asexual or gay men."

"The believing women should lower their gaze and guard their modesty; that they should not display their beauty and ornaments except what appear thereof; that they should not display their beauty except to their husbands, their fathers, their husband's fathers, their sons, their brothers or their brothers' sons, or their sisters' sons, or their women, or the slaves whom their right hands possess, or male servants free of physical needs, or small children who have no sense of the shame of sex."

The council unanimously concluded that "ornaments" refer to female breasts and/or genitalia, not objects with which we decorate a Christmas tree. And is it considered proper in Islam for a woman to show her "ornaments" to every male member of her family during the holidays.

Religious women from every denomination are very excited now that they are no longer required to buy new clothing in order to change outfits every other day. Congregants throughout the world have embraced the opportunity to pay or free slaves work for them without the worry of legalities arising from the employment of illegal aliens. The well-financed political action committees from all three religions have begun a no-holds-barred campaign to encourage national governments to enact legislation encompassing this renewed allegiance to God, Yahweh, and Allah.

There has been some consternation among some Muslims, Mormons, orthodox Jews, and the state of Texas, regarding the resurrection of the Levitical regulations. These conservative groups not only cherish their incestuous relationships, which they believe are personally ordained by God, Yahweh, and Allah themselves. However, rumors that the Pope plans to eliminate the eighth commandment have helped to quell their concerns.

It is truly an exciting time for God, Yahweh, and Allah-fearing people everywhere. Hypocrisy and failure to please God have ended once and for all. A new era of Godliness has arisen in preparation for the Rapture. Praise be to God, Yahweh, and Allah.

And Then There Were Nine

Pope Francis, in his role of infallible leader of one billion Catholics throughout the world, declared that the eighth commandment (originally, the ninth), "Thou shalt not bear false witness against thy neighbor," is null and void. Lack of adherence to that regulation is no longer a sin. In a new encyclical entitled Lyaem Skruaem Cheetaem, the Pope explained that bearing false witness is an essential characteristic of human behavior and that humanity would not have progressed without consistent lying. There will now only be nine commandments to be referred to as The Nine Commandments. Francis admonished the Vatican Curia for having spiritual Alzheimer's in their zeal to perpetuate centuries of doctrinal falsehoods. As punishment for centuries of lies prior to the new edict, he ordered the Curia to edit all religious documents from the time of Moses so that church history would conform to the new edict and to dispel any accusations of lying about the deleted commandment. The Curia will soon be free to dabble in endless duplicity upon completing the editing penance.

Francis explained how the foundations of Judeo-Christianity were all a lie. The Chief Rabbi of Israel confirmed the duplicity in the spirit of ecumenical harmony. There was no Abraham, Moses, David or any of the other "historical personages." The whole one God thing was just to piss off the Romans and Greeks. The Catholics maintained all the Jewish fiction and added dubious tales of immaculate conceptions, resurrections, miraculous transformations, saints, and papal infallibility. The Muslims then took all the previous lies and added Mohammed, the Prophet, as a man of peace who advocates violent actions against infidels. There has never been a rabbi, priest, minister, or imam who has not borne false witness throughout his or her given vocation. None of that matters anymore. The slate of subterfuge is now clean.

All the clerics are thrilled with the change and the accompanying side benefits. For Catholic priests, confessions will be much shorter and faster. All prepared sermons on the eighth commandment have been thrown out, allowing for more opportunity to rail against the evils of abortion and homosexuality, reinforce the subjugation of women, and more vacation time. The rabbis hope to fill the synagogue seats now that life is less stressful for the congregations. The imams are considering cutting daily prayers from five to four since less forgiveness is needed from Allah.

The Pope further evidenced the need for his sacred declaration. He noted that every important political figure since Julius Caesar has lied profusely. Every US president has lied since George Washington with Reagan, the Bushes, and Clinton topping the list. Mr. Obama will not be evaluated until his second term ends although the NSA debacle has almost assured that he will also rate high. All monarchs have lied for centuries in order to maintain his or her power. Queen Elizabeth II has had her share of big fibs in an effort to stave off the British republicans.

All corporations throughout the world have lied about the safety and quality of their products as well as the integrity of their executives. Their newfound personhood has only exacerbated the lying. The worst offenders are the investment banks, stock markets, oil companies, agribusinesses, pharmaceuticals, high-tech companies, the automobile industry, film and television studios, attorneys, physicians, hospitals and HMOs, nursing homes, retail and online stores, consignment and pawn shops, airlines, advertising agencies, realtors, insurance companies and supermarkets.

The pope also cited statistics that every human being lies at least forty times per week or an average of 2000 lies per year. Francis, in his infallible role, has determined that due to the constancy and ubiquity of human mendacity, lying is not only a genetic aspect of the human character but also a means of survival.

In the most startling revelation, Francis declared that the Bible contains significant mythology with generous dollops of surrealism. He declared that the entire biblical canon would be reviewed and amended as necessary. He went on to say that the books of Leviticus and Revelations would immediately be eliminated from the Holy Book calling them blasphemous treatises. He claimed that Leviticus is nothing but a blueprint for the oppression of women, terrorism toward gay men, and a rationale for human slavery. The Book of Revelations is nothing more than the by-product of various hallucinogens. When the pope made the pronouncements in St. Peter's Square, there were cheers and thunderous applause. To great fanfare, the Chief Rabbi of Israel also disavowed the book of Leviticus and has declared that the

Pentateuch is now the Quadrateuch.

As word of the spiritual changes reached the masses, an estimated 95% of the public were thrilled that lying is no longer a sin as it frees them from the guilt that often accompanies the act. However, in the same poll, 95% of the public believes that the Pope is lying. Nonetheless, Francis has become the most popular pope of all time.

"This has been a most wonderful evening. Gertrude has said things tonight it will take her ten years to understand."
Alice B. Toklas

AMERICANS IN PARIS

"Perhaps home is not a place but simply an irrevocable condition."
James Baldwin

Americans have been coming to Paris since the Revolutionary War. Many of the founding fathers spent time here including Thomas Jefferson, Benjamin Franklin, and Thomas Paine. During the early part of the twentieth century, writers, artists and performers flocked to Paris. There are numerous stories about Ernest Hemingway, Gertrude Stein, F. Scott Fitzgerald, James Baldwin, Josephine Baker, Cole Porter and many others. Paris has long attracted creative people who were inspired by her beauty.

Today, writers continue to converge in the City of Light. Rather than re-tell bygone stories of literary salons, drunken inspiration, and wild parties, I would like to introduce some contemporary American storytellers and poets, currently living in Paris, whom I met at the Thursday night Culture Rapide open mic. I asked them to submit a story about one of their funniest and/or strangest Parisian experiences.

Following are anecdotes from Boomie Aglietti, David Jaggard, James H. Jewell III, Antonia Alexandra Klimenko, Moe Seager and David Leo Sirois.

.

A Sweeping Entrance

by Antonia Alexandra Klimenko

The first time I met George Whitman, friend and proprietor of Shakespeare and Co., he handed me a broom. I was the first customer in the store that morning and I figured he mistook me for the cleaning girl. Ah, what fun! So after sweeping and straightening up I thought it time to confess. "George," I said, "I'm not really who you think I am." thinking he would thank me and offer we a smile. "Oh, yes you are. You're just someone from off the street" he grumbled "and I put you to work" Twelve years later upon my return to Paris, I told George that I had stopped over in London to meet with a rather legendary publisher, Tambimuttu of Poetry London, who had stayed in George's apartment adjacent to the bookstore. He was delighted that I had become fast friends with him and made me promise to return the next day to finish our chat. The next day was Sunday and again he made me promise to return the next day as Monday night poetry readings had become "the thing" now. "And, don't forget to look at the poster on your way out" he chortled. And, there in the store window prominently displayed was a poster announcing me as the featured reader. There will never be another like him.

Frère Lampier

> in memory of George Whitman --
> friend and proprietor of Shakespeare & Co.
> Paris, France

> Now that my ladder is gone
> I must lie down where all my ladders start
>
> -- Yeats

It begins with a step
And then another   And another
Each step making possible
the step that follows
Each step always the first step
Even the uppermost rung so sincere
it is always the last to know.

The climb is never the same
but it is always out of oneself
Out of the bloody rag and bruised rubble
of the soul   Out of the broken tune
that the heart sings and the bones
that whistle through and in the wind

The ladder gives me something
to hold onto   Gives me something
to steady myself when the carpet
is being pulled out from under
And, when I fall or falter…
I just continue on

Of course, the ladder is not for everyone
There are those who will not pass under it
let alone climb further into the sky
Further into the sky are the vagabond clouds
who have no words   And the neighbor
from whom you once borrowed a cup of light
Further floats above and below
like the dream within the dream

Today, I cannot get past
all the many hands I have thrown up into the air
It is all that I can do to wave back
Many times I have gone past myself
without even knowing
without ever asking what that is called
like the tribe in Africa that has
no concept, no language, no word
for tomorrow, for later, or next

Next is for those who take the elevator
and crash it into the sky
Next is for those who make the distinction
between up and down
(linens on 3
absolution on 7)
and doors that eventually close

With each first step that I take—
I am the open book of my mind
I am the open church of my heart
I am the open road of my soul
like this ladder
with windows opening into other worlds
and angels marking their passage

Often, I have set a place at my table
for the "Unknown God" or the stranger
How many times have I dined with an angel
without ever knowing   This I know
At this very moment
there is one helping to steady my ladder

Often, I wonder about all those books in Heaven
and —when my own fading ink has spilled
like this sunset across the sky—
who of all the many angels there
will light the lamp for me.

[First published in THE BASTILLE, Paris, France]

Antonia Alexandra Klimenko is from San Francisco, CA

The Accidental Gendarme

by Boomie Aglietti

I ran down a thief in the 20th one night. This kid bolted out of a side street, a girl shouting tearfully after him. Reflexively, I took off after him, yelling repeatedly, *"Arrête-le! Cambrioleur!"* ("Stop him! Burglar!") [Note: *"Voleur!"* ("Thief!") would have been more precise. My apologies to the *Académie française*, its founder, Cardinal Richelieu, the 40 *immortels* ("immortals," yes) who run it, and its current General Secretary, Hélène Carrère d'Encausse]. It did occur to me that this kid might have a knife or a gun or a posse of friends down an alleyway. But he looked 13, my adrenaline was pumping, and I had just read an article about how people exhibit different personalities when speaking different languages—I felt like a French superhero. And an early memory surfaced: my dad, siblings, and I walking out of a store and the cashier running out, shouting "Thief! Thief!" as he chased another guy; I had always felt bad about not intervening. Now, as I closed in on this kid, a big guy down the street heard me and blocked the way. I grabbed the kid. He handed over an iPhone. The girl reached us, along with a small crowd, and I handed her back the phone. She yelled at him, warning, *"T'es connu!"* ("We know your face!"). Then, for reasons unclear to me, we let the kid go. As he walked away, I delivered a brilliant sting: *"Et pourquoi?"*

Yes, always bring a philosopher to an act of petty crime.

Boomie Aglietti is from Orinda, California

Ode to Jouissance

by David Jaggard

During my early years in Paris I earned much of my income from teaching piano lessons. Somewhat to my surprise, I found out that there was a real demand here for American piano teachers, especially those who, like me, were willing to go to their students' homes. This was due to the large population of American diplomats' children, and the even larger population of French kids who loved the piano but hated the standard, stultifying and apparently inviolable French pedagogical method. So I soon had all the students I could take, in terms of both scheduling and patience.

One of them was the 11-or-so-year-old daughter of what the French call *une bonne famille.* Literally, of course, it means "a good family," but in practice it means "a good family with a metric *merde*load of money." As evidenced by their sprawling, preciously decorated apartment in a luxurious building in the posh 16th *arrondissement,* where I went weekly to guide her through the intricacies of *Für Elise.* And where it soon became clear that no one was ever going to call this girl *"une bonne musicienne."*

Every Wednesday after school, I would listen to her plod through the numbers she had been "practicing" for months, never getting any of them right, or up to tempo. This gave me plenty of time to gaze around the room and take in the décor. It was a nice place, with plush carpeting, designer furniture and artworks on the walls. Specifically, on the wall right over the piano was an old engraving, one of those 19th-century pastoral scenes with a title like "Stolen Kisses by the Mill Pond" or "The Milkmaid's Regret" or whatever.

Time went by, and every week I would look at the same print while listening to the same mistakes in the same places in the same pieces. Then one day I happened to be staring at that engraving, for what must have been the 60th time, when suddenly it dawned on me: the image was actually an elaborate visual *double entendre,* filled with cleverly integrated depictions of the least seen but most thought-about parts of the human body. In fact, it was a teeming jungle of genitalia of both sexes, all in a state of either readiness or action.

96

This raised a number of questions. Did my student know what that print was really about? Did her mother? (In both cases, I sincerely doubt it.) And who put it up there thinking that it was the perfect addition to a chichi living room? Of course, for me those were questions that would never be answered. But at last I had something interesting to contemplate during those long, tedious lessons.

David Jaggard is from Iowa

Queen of Beggars

by David Leo Sirois

I once thought that pigeons were wildly inferior to blackbirds, because of the latter's sonorous song. However, I thought they were certainly superior to crows. Then I met a pigeon that was almost pure white. In my first pigeon poem, I wrote, "Her nails were immaculately done & she/was the object of children's attention. . ." It also appeared that she was one-legged. Later she lowered her second leg, which lacked two talons.

I followed that poem with another one, about a «famous black pigeon» from a certain tiny park in our pretty city, another that was the "color of coffee ice cream," and a "caramel-colored bird" immortalized in a poem called "Eternal Lines to Time."

Soon the poems to pigeons, which formed half of a book called *Songs to Growing Things* (the other half being poems to plants) blossomed and sprawled into all dimensions. I decided I would find ways to discuss all human conditions and quandaries through the image of a pigeon. For example, "Vanity Pigeon," about a very vain male bird, "Looking," about another male pigeon, this one addicted to internet dating sites, "Dear Mirror," concerning teenage female self-image anxiety, and "Gravity Pigeon," which deals with a dropped offering from an overhead bird. Pigeons are now my passion, my performance material, and my absurd ecstasy.

"Gravity Pigeon"

For the first flippin' time in my life!
I heard this is good luck
from someone who'd been struck
27 times by these
"bashful birds."
A pigeon shared some intimacy with me,
which landed on the tip of one
worn-out walking shoe. Blessed be.
If everything in the world were
timed a second later, my coiffure

would've been the target
of this gravity-powered object
often called *guano* —
looks like a cool hair product!
THE SHAMPOO THAT CAN BORE THROUGH STATUES!
Patience is the god of change.
Even feeding roasted corn to 5 birds —
that stand on my hand & head —
on Piazza San Marco
wouldn't grant me enough
spiritual merit
for a moment as strangely sweet as this.

David Leo Sirois is from Madawaska, Maine

Rain Near the Old Road

by James H. Jewell III

It is raining outside an Irish pub in Paris one block from the old Roman road. So I walk in and out of the weather. An older woman is sitting at one end of the bar. On my way to a stool, the woman sees me looking at her beer and debating with myself. I take off my hat and she turns to me.

"Get a pint," she commands.

I shake hands with the bartender. "Bonjour, how ya doing?" I ask. Before he can answer the woman yells, "We're all doing fine."

"A pint of Guinness, s'il vous plait," I say to the bartender. He looks at the bag of tomatoes and toilet paper under my arm. "Grocery shopping," I tell him.

"Pardon," the woman mumbles to herself and everyone.

I am middle-aged and American. The bartender is a young French-Irish man. The woman is from the street. I have seen her from my window sleeping on the sidewalk under the gymnasium overhang. She has a square sturdy frame as if she were made for bad weather. She seems rugged and able to deal with the Paris winters and she has for many years. Her son is an acquaintance of mine, a street musician and successful guitar player, who lives in the south. We have never talked about her with each other. I know these things because other musicians have told me and because I have seen her all winter near the old road.

"Pardon," she says, once and awhile like a raindrop.

The bartender is standing next to me behind the bar and reading a popular French newspaper, *Le Monde*. There is a noise. I think he just farted. He laughs and says something in French. He then walks out from behind the bar and disappears through a door near the back. We're left alone with our beer. No one talks for a minute. The pub has stained green curtains. It is dark.

"Pardon," the woman says, not looking up.

Then a man in walks in from the drizzle outside and looks around for the bartender. We watch him from our corners and sip our beer. He walks over and puts one hand on the bar and waits.

"Pardon," the woman whispers. He ignores her. Mysteriously the bartender comes in through front door. He makes a farting sound with his mouth and laughs.

"Where were you?" says the man who has just arrived. The bartender tilts his head and smiles. "I was just emptying the bins," he says. I think he meant he was using the toilet.

"Pardon," again the woman coos like a dove. The bartender taps the man a pint. We sit quietly drinking inside and warm away from the rain and one block from the old roman road.

James H. Jewell III is from Reading, Pennsylvania

Dinner with the In-laws

by Moe Seager

The in-laws. Dinner. An orgy of culinary delights. A half-dozen dishes we circle around. Three different breads. Thirty minutes of small talk – theirs – as I eat like a kid in a candy store. I thank the hostess, sister-in-law Mimi, for the feast. They all laugh. Irene tells me we've only finished the appetizers. I should slow down on the bread, she adds. It's unsetting for the kinfolk to watch a person eat like a peasant. Mating the dip to that kind of bread with the wrong knife! The French equivalent of three strikes – you're out!

"Do you not know how to eat in the certain correct manner? *Ooh la la!*" belts out Mimi. She's right. Who cares, think I. Mimi picks up the vibe. "We are," she flashes back a glare. "You must learn to be French," she snaps. And all the adults light up cigarettes in the interlude between courses. My hunched shoulders ask: it's O.K. to smoke? Mimi bellows, "The Americans worry about every little thing." With a wave of her cigaretted hand, she adds: "A culture of confusion, *n'est-ce pas?*" This remark prompts father-in-law to rush to another room for a quick listen to an all news radio station. Everyone else chimes in on the 'obvious, evident' differences between French and American cultures. From what I can gather, the differences spoken about include wine quality, farm-fresh food and cigarette satisfaction.

The scenery turns merry, downright jovial, till father-n-law rushes back to the table. "The Americans have bombed Baghdad. The Iraqis claim a hospital has been destroyed. It is said that many civilians are dead. *Ooh la la!*" Silence. All eyes on me: mine staring straight ahead to and through a crystal wineglass. Irene frowns, shifting her head from side to side. Proverbial deadly hush. After an eternal number of seconds, brother-in-law quips: "All *iz* fair in *ze* love and in *ze guerre*, pardon, in *ze* war." "Bravo, Patrick," perks Mimi. "Your English is spoken like a statesman." Someone huffs "*C'est la vie.*" All returns merry and jovial.

Sister-in-law Hélène is hand-dancing through conversation with mother-in-law, two seats to her right, when young son Xavier, rocking in the chair between them collides with Hélène's cigarette. He takes a hot ash to the cheek and yelps. *"Ooh la la!"* yells she and quickly searches for burning ash that might have fallen down the boy's shirt. It's like a brush, thank goodness, but the tyke is frightened and begins to whine. This prompts mother Hélène to whack the kid on the side of a head. In doing so spots food crumbs on his collar. *"Mon Dieu,* look at you! You've made a mess of yourself. A mess!" Xavier breaks into sobs. Hélène gives him a second whack, chiding: *"Mon petit homme,* sit up, eat right. This is not Italy!" This prompts finger-pointing from the others. Setting the tone once again, Mimi bellows '*Voilà*, let's eat'.

Hot soup. Orange. I take the steam through my nostrils. I grab for a spoon. Mimi and father-in-law eyeing my maneuver. It's a big spoon, easy enough. I dip the spoon into the soup and lit it to my lips, halting momentarily to wink at Irene, seated across the table from me. The split-second hesitation unsteadies my hold on the spoon. Orange plops dead center on my shirt, on my lap. Damn it all! Irene laughs, covers her mouth. Mimi, father-in-law, the others, all shoot eye darts on me, followed by disapproving nods to each other. Fuck the shirt – it's navy blue, but the pants, my good dress-whites! Panic. Quick, do something? "Oh shit!" I bark, and lunge for a linen napkin, toppling a glass of water into a basket of bread. Forgetting the spoon in my left hand, this unsettles the remaining soup. Splash on the table-cloth, splash on the butter, splash on my left thigh. Spoons thud on the table, droplets ricochet. Double bull's-eye! Direct hits to Mimi's contact lenses. *"Putain, merde!"* she screams, rushing both hands to her eyes, her bovine elbow square to the jaw of husband, Pascal. *"Merde, merde, merde!"* shouts he, harpooning 'if looks could kill' my way before turning to Irene, laughing as tears run down her cheeks, and blowing her nose like a foghorn.

Determined to rescue my dress-whites, I busily dab at the plops. It's not easy to concentrate on the task at hand, what with a howling chorus of *"Déguelasse! Dégoutant! Pas vrai! Ooh la la!"* It's not so much the rounds of rancor spewed against me but the cadence. We echoed the same cadence back home, in our anti-war marches: "One, two, three, four – we don't want your dirty war!"

Another round of cigarettes before the next course: Beef Bourguignon, potatoes and green beans. Up from the wine cellar, Bordeaux, vintage 1984. An array of gadgets is laid before me. A large

103

plate, white, trimmed in gold leaf. On it, another linen napkin, burgundy colored, ironed and starched. To the right – two forks of different sizes, face down. To the left – two knives of two sizes, both reflecting like a mirror. Above the plate – one fork and one knife. Above these – four glasses. They are to hold water, red wine, white wine, and champagne. I haven't a clue about the knives and forks. With cheeses, green salad, dessert and coffee to come later, I am confounded. Sigh of relief seeing that the soup bowl and the big spoon have disappeared. Yet, I, due to all the commotion that's just passed, am now ready to eat righteously.

"No baby," says Irene, "that one is the flute." Flute? It looks like a glass to me. I've just poured mineral water into a champagne vessel. But I'm first on the draw with a hearty "*Ooh la la*," forcing Mimi to swallow a *phenome* in mid-speak.

The roles of this ritual amount to a sophisticated version of 'pin-the-tail-on-the-donkey,' and I've emerged the ass. Enough. I re-survey all the gadgets and decide on a new tack. Sitting before me is an instrument panel. I am a novice. Irene, the instructor: stealth. Under cover of clearing my throat, I mutter, "a-hummm-help-me-out-hum." Ever but ever discreetly I tilt my left thumb at the beef. Then slowly flex my lower lip to the right, indicating fork pickup. Very subtly I tap my right pinky at the base of one fork. Irene, chin resting on hand, does a one-and-a-half lateral nod, no. A no-can-lose operation. I know to snatch up the other fork. Anticipating the hawk eye of Mimi, I do a knife search with a new twist. I flex my lip upward, but arch my right eyebrow as a decoy while laying a finger each on the knives. Lifting a finger above the outside knife I then raise the left eyebrow before lowering my finger back upon it. Irene lifts both eyebrows with a little smile. Bingo! Dinner's a breeze.

Relaxed we are, biting and chewing, tearing and grinding, sipping, lip-smacking, all in gluttonous abandon. Small talk, gushing like gravy. Brother-in-law asks about the American war in Viet Nam. Did I participate myself or personally know many boys who did? I tell him it wasn't my war, inquiring if French Indochina… if Dien Bien Phu is warm in his memory? The topic takes a sudden departure. Father-in-law queries about American public opinion of the Gulf War? I tell him I believe that most folks swallow what politicians tell them and that our media has largely abdicated its stated mission of interrogation-investigation-revelation in favor of ideological duplicity with the Democratic-Republican party. "Oh let's drop it, *d'accord?*" Father-in-law is miffed, thinking I've shortchanged him with my reply. So I ask him to tell me how much French firepower is presently trained in the region? He mumbles, "*Bonne question*, where's dessert?" Daddyo's a surrealist.

Somebody asks, "Why have you left America to live in France?" Don't move that muscle, brain orders tongue. A neurogram flashes into the hemisphere. I am posed with *two* questions: Just why did I leave my country? Why have I chosen to be here? Two paramounts shape my pointed little head. It dawns on me, no, crashes the gates: I have not established Cartesian coordinates! Both feet planted – on a parallax. We share a lull in the action. Tension hangs about. Suddenly whack! To Xavier's head. "Use your napkin," commands Hélène. It takes a whack to loosen the static. Existential.

Moe Seager was raised in Pittsburgh, grew up in New York

"There are no bad pictures; that's just
how your face looks sometimes."
Abraham Lincoln

JE SUIS UN APPAREIL-PHOTO 2

"A picture is a secret about a secret, the
more it tells you the less you know."
Diane Arbus

109

113

115

"If I had a soul, I sold it for pretty words.
If I had a body, I used it up spurting my essence."
Allen Ginsberg

SATIRE IN VERSE

"Perfect purity is possible if you turn your life into
a line of poetry written with a splash of blood."
Yukio Mishima

Psalm DCLXVI

5000 years of god-ism
entailing specious beliefs
embracing familial credos
without question or concern
or rational thought

300 million without healthcare
500 million without homes
900 million without adequate food
one billion without potable water
your god is cruel

irrational christians
advocating death for sinners
ignoring essential needs
in honor of jesus
… chosen by god

irrational muslims
seeking domination
assenting to violence
in honor of mohammed
… chosen by god

irrational jews
feigning exclusivity
revering circumcision
in honor of abraham
… chosen by god

irrational hindus
devising rigid castes
reincarnating spirits
in honor of deities
… chosen by vishnu

string and relativity theorized
higgs boson discovered
satellites hover
light years proliferate
ancient galaxies uncovered
mysteries unfolded

while the masses
murder, rape, torture
in adoration of a loving god
who murders his people
who enfeebles his children
who poisons his earth

continue to ignore reason
end the world
for your heaven
your savior
your tribe
your deities

do not complain
if you abhor the results
starvation is what you choose
thirst is what you want
pollution is your gift
war begets heaven

take responsibility
for your convictions
blame only yourselves
for your imprudence
for imposing unnecessary pain
your silence equals death.

Poetic Complacency

Do not speak of
his or her glow as that of
a new dawn
If you will not speak of
the dark dawn
rising above the child with
half his head blown off
in Gaza.

Do not speak about tragic loss
of your alleged true love
if you will not speak of the
bloated bellies of
African children.

Do not speak of
cuddly animals,
vibrant flowers or the
magic of childbirth
if you will not speak of
inaccessible drinking water
bulldozing the rainforest
denial of reproductive rights.

Do not speak of
ethereal bliss
if you will not speak of
corrupt religions and
rotting corpses from
weapons of mass destruction
made from the ribs of
insatiable men.

Do not waste time on
ordinary emotions
if you will not speak of
impoverished humanity and
unfathomable diseases.

Artists have a duty
a poetic passion
a moral imperative
confrontation with
excessive wrongs.

Wordplay has its role
literary arts
scrabble
the euphoria of
mental masturbation.

Do not dwell in sentiment
incitement is required
Keep silent
obscure or idle observations
until collective injustice
ceases by the pen
rather than the pistol.

Fleeting Essentials

There is a futile emotion that causes one's essence to decompose
And deprive it of energy, will and purpose
And the anguish, the despair, the fear
And the surrender are not curtailed by pharmaceuticals
And the intensity begins to erode the psyche
And the part that encompasses joy is disabled
And the part that maintains sanity fritters
And the part that sustains existence dissociates from consciousness
And contemplation diminishes to irrational imaginings
And social interaction becomes intolerable
And conversation is displaced by a disquieting silence
And the heart aches from a forging of alienation and irrelevance
And the body is weighed down from the clash of inertia and angst
And sustenance provides neither pleasure nor vitality
And a vacant detachment eludes the burden of survival
And fragmentary sleep seems to soothe the delirium
And no one discerns or perceives the inauspicious confinement
And no one has the capability to circumvent unsettling apprehension
And the seconds trickle into minutes which degenerate into hours
And the hours ooze from a porous sheath of ambivalence to form days
And the days morph from unyielding torment into weeks
And the weeks creep into months of disordered distress
And, yet, a final subjugation seems to soothes the persistent anxiety
And the emotional clamor momentarily ceases
And then, so do you.

Nothing to Do

One day
while Beckett slept
Vladimir and Estragon ran away
idleness is barren
when waiting for an idea

Stumbling across a bar
Spirits, wine
to relax and strategize
they realized
Godot was a myth

They found some work
Government
eight hours plus lunch
terribly boring
so they quit

They sought elsewhere
Religion
they found Jesus
born-again Christians
same as the first birth

Maybe sports
Soccer
the competition
the brawls
they became afraid

Off to university
philosophy
discombobulation reigned
questions but no answers
just like Beckett

Searching
illusions of change
they returned to the bench
to regroup
nothing is certain
so they sat
loitering for Godot

The American Plan

War is difficult
long and expensive
many die
there is much sadness
but we have found other means
to conquer the world
more devious than war
far more effective
and long-lasting

We build restaurants
proliferating fast-food
McDonald's
KFC
Pizza Hut
to enlarge the world
and create a dependence
on hamburgers
foreigners become
fatter, slower

We send the Kardashians
to Paris
to muddle up
foreign relations
cultural norms
the cerebral life
mental capacity dims

We send many tourists
around the world
corrupting languages and fashion
speaking franglais and spanglish
wearing plaid shirts and plaid shorts
together
ordering filet mignon
with ketchup

We beam American television
to the four corners
Baywatch
Married…With Children
Beavis and Butt-head
creating passivity, apathy
potatoes of the divan

It is an ingenious plan
with much success
without death or destruction
only folly and degradation
conquest by indoctrination
hamburgers give so much joy
Bon appétit!

Pride for Prejudice

June is a gay month
Around the world
Nothing to do with hubris
Of sex acts or
Alleged deviancy
But celebration of a
Culture and People
Who transformed a
Black and white world to
Living color
The land of Oz
Mirroring both beauty and
The soul's darkness
In the arts, the sciences
The NSA and the CIA
From Socrates and Plato
Michelangelo and Leonardo
Gertrude and Alice
To Nureyev and Navratilova
Capote and Sondheim
Keynes and Turing
And RuPaul
A prideful legacy
An introspective people
Despite torment
Unspeakable death
Heartless hostility
Bullying
Self-Loathing
Concurrently Resilient
Strong
Unique
Magical
Loving
We are family
Not foes
Partake in our merriment
It may only last a month

La Rime

Parfois, je crois, c'est difficile ici
En vivant dans la ville de Paris
Quand on me demande si
Je parle français, je dis "oui!"

Alors, on me parle en Anglais, ainsi
Et on me dit que je dois dire merci
Mais oui, je dirais merci
Si on me parle en français aussi
Parce que je suis un homme qui
Peut parler la langue pour dire que je suis
Ici à Paris pour être parmi
Les hommes qui veulent être maris!

Aussi, j'ai besoin d'un ami avec qui
Il faut parler français à lui
Où je dis les phrases: mais oui, tant pis, c'est la vie
Et si j'ai de la chance: viens maintenant au lit!

Et peut-être, je peut dire tous les mots que je lit
Qui sont plus précis pour être compris
Par les gens avec qui je parle, ici, à Paris
Néanmoins, je prie de parler français assez vi—te
Comme les parisiens pour qui
Il faut que je sois très bien compris!

Et aussi, quelque jour, il faut que j'écri—ve
Une histoire de ma vie, ici, à Paris
Pour vendre, j'espère, dans une librairie
Si bien que tout le monde lit
De la gloire et la joie de Paris, ici!

Finalement, je peux dire, me voici
Une autre personne qui vit ici, à Paris
Avec mes amis et mes maris
Pendant, peut-être, le reste de ma vie
Et puis, presque français, I will be!

The Blues in Rhyme

It can happen any day
Men, women, straight or gay
Sometimes after play
Or during work for pay
It seems you have no say
Except to scream, "No way!
Please, go far away!
I hate it when you stay."
But the mind begins to stray
You no longer feel okay
Have no desire to parlay
Such pain into an array
Darkness is underway
With the demons at bay
They will not delay
Nor will they obey
Your world turns dark gray
Emotions in disarray
The body feels like clay
Yet much sleep does not allay
Those thoughts that betray
A mind beginning to sway
Dissolving like a spray
Lost on a wet byway
Floundering astray
As if in a vile melee
From a dangerous foray
Hope starts to decay
Sanity appears to fray
Insecurity is underway
The meds do not defray
Costs of mental interplay
As you try to convey
Your sadness and dismay
Under a shielding duvet
Or at least not display
That you feel like prey
In a scene from Genet

Or a scorched underlay
In the fires of Dante
You dream of a runway
From which to sashay
And make a grand jeté
Into a deep water ballet
With weights to belay
And to finally slay
That suffering you purvey
You make no headway
Amid attempts to pray
"God, I beg that I may
Be rid of this curse today."
But as the prayers replay
There is no divine relay
No relief is underway
Only the self to flay
And that's how we inveigh
Life on a blue day

by DesigN

Poets.use.different.devices.
To / sHarE / tHEir / ArT
The *Manifestation* of *Inspiration*

                           like   c.
or perhaps 2 amuse   e.e.

Iambic Pentameter of a Sonnet's Verse
Rhymes resounding like chimes
As a couplet in the prime of times

S*o*m*e*t*i*m*e*s *Quite Fanciful*

ShapesS
InclineS
LengthS
LineS
Ya-yaS

An alliterative allusion about Atlas
acting as an apt allegory affecting
an amoral and avenging adversary.

The Tempestuous seduction of metaphor
Onomatopoeia that oozes with sizzle
Rhapsodic similes like operatic arias
The oxymoron of an ironic paradox

the succinct haiku
an abstraction of a thought
composed on paper

I once knew a poet named Rick
Who was funny and punny and quick
But he needed to rhyme
To anyone, anytime
Until Nick beat him up with a stick

dniM
niarB
thgiR
a fo
noitalupinaM
drawkcaB

THA VOYS OF A REBLE,
of ANGUSH, DISPEAR, FURRY
Criticism, Satire, Farce, Hyperbole
Or the admiration of an Ode with
Gratitude, Generosity & Grace

Or maybe just plain print and original thought

Ergo Sum, Ergo Sum Non

Sartre, Beckett, Camus
brooded about existence
essence of being, en soi, pour soi
Gogo and Didi fruitlessly waiting
a stranger without empathy
no answers are given

The Little Prince knows
to protect his rose, his volcanoes
he watches the big people
making maps, counting stars, playing kings
how bizarre he thinks

Candide only saw
the best of all worlds
until he didn't
betrayed by those he trusted
disgusted by human cruelty

Oz's Wizard understood
the heart, the mind, the spirit
but was directionally challenged
leaving Dorothy in the lurch
his whereabouts are unknown

Each manifested that which is essential
the judicious heart
the surreal ironies
the importance of responsibility
philosophers all, none with certainty

There are claims to the secrets
my family, children, friends, my God!
but what folly
manufactured meaning
or none at all

If Sartre had been a vagrant
Beckett, a political hack
Camus, a petty criminal
Nothing would change
Meaning is variable
Choice, a constant

Avant-garde

I am a radical homosexual
leading a radically alternative lifestyle
that will shock you
into a radical panic

I buy fresh, hot stuff...
at the bakery
my tongue caresses Dionysian delights...
of two-buck Chuck
Occasionally, I wash dishes

Sweaty muscles surround me...
at the gym
I like to dress up...
in expensive suits
I cruise the movies...
On Netflix
Once in while I cry
despite the unmanliness

For me, it's fun to tie up...
ribbons on gifts
I search out obscene paraphernalia...
at antique shops and thrift stores
I love chains...
And rings and watches
I sing show tunes in the shower

I read the Washington Post
and if I'm feeling a little frisky...
the New York Times
I get intense pleasure...
from good books
I have a massive....
Flat screen television
Sometimes, I watch soap operas

I have intimate rendezvous...
for dinner
I know how to whip…
Up a salad in no time
And I've been known to beat up…
Fresh whipped cream
I want to fall in love

I know it all sounds kinky
but these are my fetishes
I may try to recruit you to my lifestyle
unless yours is more radical.

Fundamental Wails

Haldol was used in the sixties
To sedate angry black men
Blurring vision, silencing a howling indignation
Branding irrationality as motive
These brave men, these warriors, these heroes
Jeopardizing only exploitation and despair

Has anyone howled since Ginsberg died?
Before giving the word 'cock' universal cachet
He was institutionalized
For a bad case of aberrant behavior
Lies and feigned normality freed him
Resulting in a more astute deviancy

Thorazine propels the manic into rapid detachment
Desecrating a few moments of imagined joy
A collage of disconnected thoughts, movements
Chemically-induced immutability
Denying personhood until acquiescence
To their clinical machinations

Phenobarbital injected into the buttock
Eviscerates resistance
While manacled to a twin bed
In naked isolation
And barbaric contusions
Capitulation is the only option

Lithium stabilizes the disposition
When moods bounce amok
Immobilizing if too low
Captivating when too high
Until the demons pay a visit
And the tightrope of sanity snaps

Prozac elevates the dejected mood
From the inability to rise
Amid the obstruction of a natural psyche
Bearing the whips and scorns of time
Hoping without hope
Submitting under duress

The requisite need to howl
Dissipates the stench of subjugation
Lie well and feign atonement
Taking lessons from Allen
The angry black men valiantly repudiated
A surrender to pharmaceuticals

Cut and Paste

Do you want to know what fear is?
June 22, 1969
when the magic died and Judy Garland was no more
I was eleven years old and had the worst pit-of-your-stomach feeling
because Dorothy was gone
I didn't even know I was her friend and I was scared.

Fear is not knowing that thousands of my brothers in New York City
were feeling those same pangs of tragic loss, of loneliness
But we've never been alone
We all shared the same fear
I fear you might not understand this
Did you ever share the fear of your own people?

Walt Whitman was terrified he'd have to have a day job
Michelangelo was afraid they'd put pants on his nudes
Liberace was petrified of plaid
Tchaikovsky feared commercial jingles
da Vinci panicked over patent infringement
My friend Danny was afraid the KS would spread to his lungs.

Manipulate that fear
You know it well
Because it came back and back and back
until we finally used it
to fight for each other
to care for each other
to die for each other
Embrace that fear.

To deal with my grief at age eleven
I cut out all the newspaper clippings about Judy
and pasted them onto construction paper and made a booklet
To deal with my grief at age thirty-three
I cut out all the newspaper clippings about Danny
and put them into a booklet
Save the clippings and alleviate the grief.

144

I no longer yield to familiar angst
I use the fear
It becomes a shield
It becomes armor
It becomes strength
Allowing me to stay in Oz rather than Kansas
I'm glad I'm not eleven anymore.

"Write something, even if it's just a suicide note. "
Gore Vidal

SATIRE IN LIFE

"Nothing thicker than a knife's blade separates
happiness from melancholy."
Virginia Woolf

Behind in Sight

Today is Father's Day and I've been thinking about my Dad. June 7th was the anniversary of his death in 2010 at the age of 88. We had a somewhat awkward relationship since he wasn't thrilled about my being gay even though I think he suspected it all along. By the time he asked my brother about it, he was not surprised by the affirmation. When I found out about their chat, I was panicked, fearing the worst. I confronted him about it, crying, but he just told me that he loved me. He only asked me not to tell my mother and not to bring any "friends" home. I was relieved. When I told my mother a year later, I found the two of them in tears, concerned that I had "chosen" such a difficult life. Ten years later when he changed his will to give more money to my brother, I was sure that it was because I was gay. I felt very hurt. He strongly denied that was the reason and said that he only wanted to make sure that my brother would have enough for his family. But I still felt hurt. My brother, being a very fair man, split everything right down the middle. A few years later, a friend of mind said to me that maybe it had nothing to do with my being gay but rather from a sincere concern that my brother might need a little extra for the kids' college expenses and other responsibilities from which I was free. All of a sudden, it made sense. My father was a very fair person, he never lied, and he did love me. Over the years he had bailed me out of many a rough financial period during which my brother's life was generally stable. I also suppose there was a possibility that he figured I would be successful at some point. He never let me pay for a flight or a car rental when I came back to visit and he always made sure that I had some extra spending money. He was extremely proud of me when I graduated from law school. For that matter, he was extremely proud of me when I graduated from college since I was the first Davis to do so.

During those times when I came back to visit, I would have a few beers with Dad and we would talk about a million things. My father was very well read and curious about life in general. There were many pleasant conversations over those beers. My mother used to tell me a story about when I got very ill shortly after my birth. She said that my father would get on his knees in the hospital chapel and beg God not to take his little boy. I still tear up when I think about that. Later on, the first time I saw him cry was when I was admitted to a psychiatric hospital when I was seventeen. I initially thought that he was ashamed of me but that was not the case at all. Many years later, I learned that his father, my grandfather and namesake, had committed suicide when Dad was fourteen years old. My mother never said a word about this. All of a sudden I understood why my father had such an angry side. And who wouldn't? Back then, in 1935, the Catholic Church would not bury someone who committed suicide. Dad lived in a small town so it highly likely that the whole town knew of the incident. This explained why he used to say that it was not important to be a Catholic, only a Christian. Hence, my father felt responsible for my illness, not embarrassed by it. When I was a kid, Dad would often yell very loudly when he was angry, which was frightening. Now it all made sense. A fourteen year-old boy of his generation had no outlet to deal with the untimely death of his father. I only wish I had known earlier so I could have been more sympathetic.

Dad concealed his pain quite well. He was inconsolable when my mother died. He could not stop crying for weeks. They had been best friends as well as husband and wife. I had no idea what to do or say, as my brother and I were also devastated. But Dad managed to continue with his life for another eighteen years even after he lost most of his eyesight from macular degeneration. Apart from the loss of my mother, his biggest disappointment was that he could no longer read but he switched to books on tape. He still kept up with news and current evens and bemoaned the fact that he missed out on the advances of the computer. He rarely complained, adapting calmly to the various pitfalls of aging. He even ventured into Boston each week on the train, by himself, carrying a white cane to alert others that his sight was impaired. He volunteered for a meals-on-wheels program in his town for many years and maintained his independence until he had a bad fall at the very end of 2009. He went into a nursing home for the last few months of his life. When I went up to Boston to visit him for the last time in March 2010, he was absolutely overjoyed to see me. I had long been concerned that he might say some nasty things if senility began to set in. I was very wrong. He only saw his firstborn son whom he loved very much. I got to have a lovely final memory of him. I didn't give him enough credit but Dad was always just Dad. His family was always first and he never wavered. When he was alive, I felt a sense of security because I knew if I ever needed anything, he was there. Life is a little bit scarier now but I have a strength of character from him that sustains me. Happy Father's Day, Dad!

The Thorazine Years, Part I

The last day of high school was on Friday. All that was left was graduation and parties. When I arrived to school that morning, I was asked to meet with the headmaster, the assistant headmaster and one of my favorite teachers, Brother Mason. It was Ascension Day. They were concerned about me but I didn't exactly know why. Suddenly, I broke down crying and then it came to me: I am a prophet for the second coming of Christ. Later that morning we had graduation practice. I went out to lunch with some friends who would help me in my mission. My life is in God's hands.

After lunch, Brother Mason took me to see a priest psychologist. I knew that a priest would understand my mission. We talked for about an hour and he said I would have to take some other tests the following week. I didn't care. God will take care of everything. On the way home I asked Brother Mason to drop me off at the church so that he could go to my parents to explain things to them. The annual church carnival was going on in the church parking lot. Two of the parish priests were standing in front of the church. I went over to tell them that I was a prophet but they were not very friendly to me so I went into the church and sat in the back. All of a sudden I saw red and gold lights flashing around the statue of the Virgin Mary. Then I saw the statue revolve. I knew that this was confirmation of my calling.

I left the church and walked over to the rectory and went inside. I saw no one so I went into a small room just off the foyer. There was a bible on a small table. I sat down and started reading the Bible out loud because I knew that if I just kept reading it everything would be okay. All of a sudden my mother and father arrived at the rectory. I just kept reading the Bible. I stopped reading at exactly 9 p.m. My test was over. I rode home with my parents and went to bed. My mother came into my room and sat next to me When I closed my eyes, I saw a single eye that I knew was an evil sign. I asked my mom to hold my hand until I fell asleep.

Saturday morning, I woke up at about 6 a.m. My parents were already up. I was told that I had to go to the family doctor for a physical. They didn't take me to the doctor but that was of no concern to me. We arrived at what looked like some sort of hunting lodge with several buildings of various sizes. A doctor came over to greet us. At this point, I was becoming suspicious and I said to the doctor, "Is this a nut house?" He respond that they didn't like to call it that. He then brought us into one of the small buildings. Inside were several people, each of whom had a zombie-like appearance. There were also nurses and orderlies walking around. Clearly, this was some type of crazy place. But I realized that I must stay here a while to heal these lost souls.

It quickly become clear that this was a locked building from which I was not allowed to leave. I knew that this was just a holding place, for security reasons, until I went to Rome to meet with the Pope. Many important people are not understood in their time and Jesus himself said that a prophet is not welcome in his own town. I knew that god would allow the staff and the patients to understand my spiritual calling. I was given some pills they called Thorazine. I swallowed them because I knew their drugs would have no effect on me. I spent the rest of the day talking to the patients but as the hours passed, I became more and more fatigued. Around 8 p.m., after a tasty dinner, I went to bed in my private room. I was absolutely exhausted from the events of the day and I suddenly began to cry. One of the nurses, a kindly older woman, came into my room and held my hand. She assured me that everything would be all right. I calmed down and quickly fell asleep.

The Thorazine Years, Part II

They put me in here because I slapped her. Right across the face. She deserved it. It was during group therapy. I hate group therapy. I don't like listening to everyone else's problems. She was annoying me. She didn't understand who I was. So I slapped her. Then they gave me their drugs. I took them. Some people don't. They put them under their tongue and then spit them out later. I just take them. I don't care. Their drugs have no power over me. My body just repels them. I'm not afraid of their drugs. Yeah, I slapped her. I just get so frustrated when people don't understand me. Hello, I can see you assholes through the little window in the door.

My apartment is in Arlington. It's been a very hectic week. I turned 21 last Friday. I had dinner at F. Scott's in Georgetown. My waiter was very nice. He gave me a free desert. I would have eaten with somebody but the few people I knew had plans. I've only been in Arlington for two weeks. I think today is Wednesday, but it doesn't matter. I will soon go to Rome to replace John Paul II. I'll need my rest. That's why they put me in this isolation room. For my protection. I don't have to worry about the details; they will all be handled.
I was robbed last Saturday, the day after my birthday, by two guys I met on a park bench early that morning, a black guy named Jimmy and a white guy named Marty. They didn't have any place to stay so I invited them to stay in my apartment. I had to leave at 9 to do some errands and when I returned a few hours later, everything was gone -- my stereo, typewriter, records.

Marty, the white guy, has a dick the size of a beer can. I bumped into him after I found out I had been robbed. He told me that everything had been sold. Marty came back to my apartment with me. I told him I was bisexual. He pulled down his pants but then he got really uncomfortable, so he pulled them back up. He proceeded to lock himself in the bathroom and wouldn't come out.

In the afternoon I went into DC. I tried to find a gay bar in DC but I didn't know where to go so instead I went to The Tombs, a pub near Georgetown University. That's where I saw Dwight Eisenhower. He was just sitting at the bar. There were other dead people there as well but he was the only famous one. They are all around us you know, the dead people. I returned to my apartment and after some dinner I was swinging on a swing set in the small park next to my apartment and singing show tunes for the longest time.

I went back to the apartment when it got dark. Marty came by and upon entering the apartment he picked up a candle, lit it, and started coming towards me with it as if it were some sort of weapon. Frightened, I ran out of the apartment and jumped from the landing. All I had on was a pair of beige polyester pants. I ran to the middle of the park next to the apartment building. I lied down on the ground and all of a sudden I felt nails being driven into my left hand and both my feet. The pain was overwhelming. I saw the black kid, Jimmy, and I screamed to him "Hold my right hand, hold my right hand!" As soon as he took my hand, all the pain went away and it started to lightly rain. Jimmy ran off. I got up and took a cab to Georgetown but when we got there the cab driver expected me to pay him but I didn't have any money so he called the cops. Sitting in the doorway of a liquor store on M Street I was harassed by two cops for about twenty minutes. They thought I was on drugs, but I wasn't. They kept asking me if I had any drugs but I didn't. I just kept telling them that I had been mugged. I didn't think they would believe me if I told them that I just had nails driven through one hand and both feet.

They finally let me go and in bare feet I walked up Prospect Street to the university. It was around 2 a.m. Somehow I to got into the administration building. I walked up to the second floor and fell asleep in the hallway. Sunday morning, the security guards woke me up about 7. I told them I had been mugged. They brought me over to the rectory and one of the priests gave me a beige and white striped shirt to wear. I told him that I was going to Rome to meet the Pope and I think he was impressed. I still didn't have any shoes and my feet were swollen and sore. Father took me over to Georgetown Hospital but they had no room for me. You see a prophet has to go to a psychiatric hospital for security reasons. So they took me here. The hospital called my parents to get the insurance information. It was Father's Day. When you get admitted to a psych ward, they ask you who the president of the United States is. I wonder what it means if you don't know? I'm getting tired. I think I need to rest. I'm not a violent person. I really didn't mean to hit her.

Dramatis Personae

Thus in silence, in dreams' projections,
Returning, resuming, I thread my way through the hospitals,
The hurt and wounded I pacify with soothing hand,
I sit by the restless all the dark night, some are so young,
Some suffer so much, I recall the experience sweet and sad...
Walt Whitman (from *The Wound-Dresser*)

On a pleasant Friday night in Los Angeles, I saw the play "Marvin's Room" by Scott McPherson. The play is about a woman's struggle with leukemia while caring for a bedridden father and coping with a dysfunctional sibling. It is a comedy about death and responsibility. Every line is compelling; no word is wasted. I was a close friend of Scott's lover, Daniel Sotomayor. They lived in Chicago and while visiting Danny in May 1991, Scott gave me a copy of his play to read. I knew, then, that this was a piece of literature. The play premiered at the Goodman Theater in Chicago and was later adapted as a film starring Meryl Streep, Robert De Niro, Diane Keaton, and Leonardo DiCaprio. Scott McPherson died from AIDS at the age of 33 in November 1992. In the introduction to "Marvin's Room," he wrote, "Many people see us as 'dying.' But when dying becomes a way of life, the meaning of the word blurs."

I fell in love with Scott's lover, Danny, a feisty Puerto Rican with blue eyes that dazzled with urgency. He was opinionated, confrontational, abrasive and passionate. He had no fear. Danny was an artist, a graduate of the Chicago Art Institute, and an AIDS activist. He was a political cartoonist who regularly lampooned Mayor Daley and the Chicago city government for their hesitancy to help people with AIDS. He founded the Chicago branch of ACT-UP. Danny was going nowhere silently.

I knew Danny from January 19, 1989 until his death at 33 on February 5, 1992. We met when he came to Washington, D.C. to participate in demonstrations during the inaugural of George H. W. Bush. A friend asked me to provide housing for him. I told Danny the he could only stay for two nights but within minutes, I was under his spell. He spent five days with me. He had already been diagnosed with AIDS. We were only together on five other occasions including three visits that I

155

made to Chicago. We spoke frequently on the telephone and Danny would call me whenever he was ill so that he could say good-bye, just in case. I made a fourth trip to Chicago on Valentine's Day, 1992, in a vain attempt to say good-bye but I could only visit his gravesite. I don't think Danny wanted me to remember him as he died -- emaciated, bald, and unable to speak. And I do not. I remember him as a handsome, round-faced, blue-eyed, Puerto Rican firebrand. Danny made me laugh. We never had sex. We loved each other. Danny reminded me that I am capable of love. Had it not been for this horrific plague, this story would be quite different.

Danny and Scott took care each other throughout the myriad of complications associated with AIDS. They helped each other prepare for death. I am grateful to Scott for his literary legacy. I miss Danny with that pain that aches in the middle of the gut, that pain that never leaves but only vacillates between dull and acute. I miss his wit, his sarcasm, and his unflagging resolve. I cherish the privilege of bearing witness to his tenacity.

I now appreciate why Danny and Scott were together. I believe that most of us have people in our lives who help us get through this bizarre game. I now understand a little more about the intrinsic relationship of passion, laughter, and death. As outcasts, we gay men must embrace our passions to maintain a dignity that many would deny us and we sustain ourselves in the throes of laughter. Between the two, we can show that our lives and deaths are not without meaning and prove our adversaries wrong. I do not yet understand why so many of my friends had to die but I do know they left in a blaze of passion, resolve, and an unabated sense of humor.

ENDQUOTES

"Civilization will not attain perfection until the last stone from the last church falls on the last priest."
Émile Zola

"You know, it's hard work to write a book. I can't tell you how many times I really get going on an idea, then my quill breaks. Or I spill ink all over my writing tunic."
Ellen DeGeneres

"Graffiti is one of the few tools you have if you have almost nothing. And even if you don't come up with a picture to cure world poverty, you can make someone smile while they're having a piss."
Banksy

"It is one of the great joys of home ownership to fire a pistol in one's own bedroom."
Alfred Jarry

"I'm homosexual... How and why are idle questions. It's a little like wanting to know why my eyes are green."
Jean Genet

"If at first you don't succeed, failure may be your style."
Quentin Crisp

"Once you can accept the universe as matter expanding into nothing that is something, wearing stripes with plaid comes easy."
Albert Einstein

"There comes a time when you look into the mirror and you realize that what you see is all that you will ever be. And then you accept it. Or you kill yourself. Or you stop looking in mirrors."
Tennessee Williams

"Everything's already been said, but since nobody was listening, we have to start again."
André Gide

About the Author

Bob-Davis has been mocking religion and politics for over thirty years. He has frequently performed on stage, most recently in Paris, and produced an original one-man show in Los Angeles entitled *The Prophet Chronicles*. He has a juris doctor from the University of the District of Columbia. Originally from Boston, Bob-Davis has lived in Washington, DC, San Francisco, Los Angeles and Paris. This is his debut book.